lessons in
WINE SERVICE
from
CHARLIE
TROTTER

lessons in
WINE SERVICE
from
CHARLIE
TROTTER

Edmund O. Lawler

TEN SPEED PRESS
Berkeley | Toronto

Ten Speed Press
PO Box 7123
Berkeley, California 94707
www.tenspeed.com

Distributed in Australia by Simon and Schuster Australia, in Canada by Ten Speed Press
Canada, in New Zealand by Southern Publishers Group, in South Africa by Real Books,
and in the United Kingdom and Europe by Publishers Group UK.

Cover and text design: Toni Tajima
Text production: Colleen Cain
Project manager: Rochelle Smith
Special contributor: Conrad Reddick

Library of Congress Cataloging-in-Publication Data
Lawler, Ed.
    Lessons in wine service from Charlie Trotter / Edmund Lawler.
        p. cm.
    Summary: "A guide for current and aspiring wine professionals to the art
and business of creating and running a successful restaurant wine program
from renowned restaurateur Charlie Trotter"—Provided by publisher.
    Includes bibliographical references and index.
    ISBN-13: 978-1-58008-905-0 (alk. paper)
    ISBN-10: 1-58008-905-4 (alk. paper)
    1. Wine service. 2. Charlie Trotter's (Restaurant) I. Trotter, Charlie.
II. Title.
    TX925.L35 2008
    641.2'2—dc22
                                        2008009388

Printed in China
First printing, 2008

1 2 3 4 5 6 7 8 9 10 — 12 11 10 09 08

CONTENTS

FOREWORD

C harlie Trotter is an extraordinary chef in many regards; not the least among his many talents is his carefully acquired knowledge of matching food and wine. As his interest in wine has grown, so has the restaurant's wine program. Over the years, Charlie Trotter's restaurant has devoted a great deal of its ample resources to its wine program in terms of both the cellar and the sommelier talent.

The restaurant opened with a modest investment mainly in French country wines and a small, outstanding selection of California wines. Dan Duckhorn and Randall Grahm were among the first winemakers to be honored with a winemaker dinner at Charlie Trotter's; in Randall's case, only a few weeks after the opening in 1987. It was clear even from the very beginning that wine was going to be a vital component of Charlie Trotter's. Over the years, such illustrious estates and producers as Angelo Gaja, May-Eliane de Lencquesaing (Pichon-Lalande), Anthony Barton (Léoville Barton), Château Latour, Lalou Bize-Leroy (Domaine Leroy), Marcel Guigal, Hubert Trimbach, and Marcel Deiss have been featured or have presented their wines here.

In addition to the list of famous names, the most noteworthy aspect of this program is the role that flexibility in the kitchen plays at Charlie Trotter's. Not every chef is so committed to the integration of food and wine that he or she will alter dishes on the spot to complement an unexpected wine selection. Even restaurants with an extensive financial investment in a wine cellar often have a menu or a staff that isn't connected with the wine list. The mark of a truly great program in a great restaurant doesn't really lie in the number of pages in the wine list, but in the way the food and the wine list connect with the guests. This is by far the hallmark of a great wine program that is built on a service platform!

A great wine program first of all needs a great clientele: a guest list of people eager to explore new worlds of both food and wine. Next it needs a highly creative chef, who not only is focused on the craft of his own cuisine but also understands how it is enjoyed in the context of wine. Wine is in effect a sauce, but one that doesn't come from the chef's stove. Yet the flavor of wine does affect one's perception of the food consumed with it, just as the food affects the way a wine tastes. This is a simple truth, an important realization that many chefs do not acknowledge in their work. Hence the importance of creativity in the kitchen to be able to come up with unique changes on the spur of the moment to make a dish or an entire menu work with the wine when the wine was selected first. Finally, a great wine program needs a wine list that is selected to favor the palette of flavors used by the chef. An important thing to remember is that the wine is fixed, but the chef can always slightly alter a dish to complement the wine selection of his guest.

The glue that holds this triad together is the sommelier. First the sommelier finds out the wine preferences or even the food preferences of the guests, which helps to determine whether food or wine is the higher priority. This allows the waiter and the sommelier to work together with the most appropriate selection of both food and wine for the table. Then the sommelier is the messenger who brings the news of the guests' wine selection, menu preferences, expectations, and even the mood of the table back to the kitchen and allows a truly talented chef to modify the seasoning and even the way a plate is composed to make the total experience of food and wine a seamless concert.

This last element has been another great strength of Charlie Trotter's. The wine service has been led here by a long line of inventive and knowledgeable Master Sommeliers, including myself, followed by Joseph Spellman, who gained his Master Sommelier credentials while working at Trotter's. There were even two great sommeliers, later to become masters, to come out of Charlie's brief first tenure in Las Vegas: Steve Geddes and Ken Fredrickson. In Chicago, Jason Smith, Brian Cronin, and Serafin Alvarado, too, became masters under the tutelage of Charlie's wine service regimen. Today Conrad Reddick, still a future master, leads the team confidently.

Not only must the sommeliers here demonstrate that they are actively studying their craft, but the waitstaff too must attend a weekly wine meeting and tasting and learn from the sommeliers at the preservice meeting each day about the wine that will be matched to a new dish on the tasting menu. Thus Charlie Trotter's has all the elements in place for an exceptional wine and food experience: the receptive clientele, the creative chef, the beautifully selected wine list, and the sommeliers and waitstaff—and even the brigade—trained to understand how the cuisine and the wine work together with the needs of the guest. Above all else, it is Charlie's own passion for and commitment to a complete dining experience that has nurtured the restaurant's wine program over the years. This restaurant has evolved to a level of expertise in wine service that has become an example of excellence for the world. Twenty years after the founding of Charlie Trotter's, there are more than a few chefs who have followed his example, and I do believe that in the next twenty there will be many more. And I hope that this exhaustively detailed volume will inspire more than a few of them to follow his path.

—Master Sommelier Larry Stone

INTRODUCTION

A mid the warm wood and exposed brick of the dining room of
the Rubicon, a storied wine destination in San Francisco's
financial district, nearly forty of the nation's top sommeliers gathered to honor restaurateur Charlie Trotter. "I'm a sommelier trapped
in a chef's body," he confided.

But Trotter wasn't just preaching to the choir that evening in
December 2006. He has a deep appreciation for wine and the intricacies of its service. The famously fastidious, hard-charging chef is
well known for improvising a dish for the sake of the wine. Unlike
a plate of food, wine comes in a bottle; it's fixed. Trotter is proud of
his backward, almost sacrilegious approach to wine and food pairing: pick the wine, and the dish will be adjusted accordingly. That's
certainly not the style of the great chefs of Europe.

Opened in 1987, Trotter's eponymous Chicago restaurant is
built in equal parts on its food, its wine, its ambience, and the element that ties it all together—its service, which is as intuitive as it
is precise. It's been a wildly successful formula for both the chef and
his restaurant.

HONORS AND ACCOLADES

Over the years, the James Beard Foundation has awarded its version
of the Oscar to Trotter's for being the top restaurant and having the

nation's most outstanding wine service, the best overall service, and the best chef. The readers of the *Wine Spectator* have twice voted Trotter's the best restaurant in the world for wine and food. The list of five-star and five-diamond accolades goes on and on, although Trotter rarely mentions them.

There is one distinction, however, that he is quick to offer. The only two Americans to have been named the world's number one sommelier in French wines and spirits at the International Sommelier Grand Prix in Paris have both pulled corks at his restaurant: Larry Stone and Joseph Spellman.

They were both at Rubicon that evening as the American chapter of the Court of Master Sommeliers, a British-based organization dedicated to elevating the quality of beverage service, tipped its cap to Trotter with its first-ever Frederick L. Dame Award to honor individual accomplishments in the food and wine industry. The Court awards three levels of certification. The highest and most coveted is the Master Sommelier or MS.

Stone earned his MS in 1987, the same year he triumphed in Paris. At Rubicon, Stone, dapper in a suit and his trademark bow tie, recounted an illuminating exchange between him and Trotter in the early days of the restaurant: Stone had raced back into the kitchen to report breathlessly to Trotter that a table had just ordered a rare bottle of Château Mouton Rothschild. It wasn't necessarily a moment to celebrate, because the guests had also ordered a lobster dish.

A first-growth Bordeaux and a plate of lobster would be an odd combination. But on the fly, Trotter sauced the lobster to accommodate the wine. It was an inspired marriage of food and wine. That's the way it's always been at Trotter's: the food can be changed to complement the wine.

PARTNERS IN PAIRING

Trotter loved Stone's story, as it reminded him that a chef is only as good as his sommelier. He credited his wine specialists for their intense attention to detail and extraordinary diligence in reporting to the kitchen a particular wine's nuance to help him craft, each evening, smart food and wine pairings that have become the hallmark of his restaurant. It's that kind of in-the-moment spontaneity that has made Trotter's synonymous with great wine and exquisite wine service.

But there's more to Trotter's wine program than an unconventional interplay between food and wine. Trotter assigns four staffers to his wine service team and lavishes it with resources he likens to a doctor's bag from which a physician can draw just the right device or medication to make things right for a patient. His sommeliers' operating platform is an 1,800-selection wine list—representing wine regions from around the world—that is the envy of the industry.

Expertise extends beyond the wine team. Every member of Trotter's twenty-person front-of-the-house staff is trained to pour and describe wine. The restaurant's wine cellars are so pristine that they could pass for an exhibit at the Smithsonian, and the expensive Riedel stemware speaks to the high regard the restaurant has for its wine program and the guests who reap the benefits. Elegance comes with a price, however: Trotter estimates the restaurant breaks about $50,000 worth of the delicate stemware each year.

The restaurant's reverence for wine is underscored by a nearly floor-to-ceiling wine bin in the soaring foyer of Trotter's hundred-year-old brownstone. A glass-enclosed wine storage area accents one of the second-floor dining rooms, and a display of the restaurant's collection of large-format bottles always stops guests in their tracks in Trotter's studio kitchen and dining room in an adjoining brownstone.

The sommeliers can step into a kitchen whose staff will instinctively respond to any request to adjust a dish so that it complements the wine. They are assiduously and extensively trained in the names of wine and their provenance and the intricacies of wine service. The sommeliers in turn take the lead role in educating and training the front-of-the-house staff on the finer points of wine and wine service.

SUPPORTING THE CAUSE

Fred Dame, a founder and board member of the American chapter of the Court of Master Sommeliers, says the award named in his honor was given to Trotter for his long record of support for his wine service team. Dame notes how Trotter defrays the cost of courses and exams sponsored by the Court and how he grants staffers time off to take the courses and exams. Dame also notes that Trotter sees to it that his staff tastes a repertoire of wine, which enhances their ability to recognize wines in blind tastings. "You would be hard-pressed to find another restaurateur in this country who does more for his wine professionals than Charlie Trotter," Dame says.

Serafin Alvarado, who like Spellman earned his MS while working at Trotter's, flew in from Chicago to toast his former boss that evening in San Francisco. Brian Cronin, who earned his MS after leaving Trotter's, was also there. So were Conrad Reddick and Molly Wismier, the restaurant's current senior sommeliers, who inherited the legacy of the restaurant's wine program that has employed or helped produce five Master Sommeliers, an unparalleled distinction in the restaurant industry. (Master Sommelier Jason Smith, another Trotter's alumnus, was unable to attend that evening, although we meet him later in this book.)

Reddick and Wismier, who both worked previously as sommeliers in Chicago fine dining restaurants, relish the opportunity to meet the intense demands of heading the Trotter's wine program and to take it to a higher level. We'll encounter them frequently throughout the book as they describe the program, train the staff, serve the wine, buy it, bin it, taste it, and learn all they can about it through research and winery visits.

THE SECRETS OF THE TEMPLE

In the chapters that follow, we will learn how Trotter's meticulously trains its staff through role playing, drills on technical service, wine tastings, and teaching about the fine art of pairing wine with food.

Service team members are as familiar with the food as the twenty chefs in the back of the house who prepare the cuisine. The sommeliers have a deft touch for helping pair the wine with the food. Or is it the food with the wine?

We will go on the road with Charlie's sommeliers to see how their wine education is advanced through winery visits and meetings with industry leaders and experts. We will visit the cellars at Trotter's and learn how the sommeliers manage a $2 million wine inventory and create and maintain a world-class wine list. We will spend time in the dining room where the fast-paced ballet of service unfolds each evening.

We will drop in on preservice meetings in which the service team reflects on the previous evening's service and plots service for the night ahead. We will meet many of Trotter's former sommeliers, who reflect on their experiences in the restaurant that's long been synonymous with superlative wine service.

This book is intended to be a guide for people in wine service, including sommeliers, wine stewards, beverage managers, wine retailers, wine importers and distributors, dining room managers, bartenders, restaurant owners and operators, winemakers, wine buyers, cellar masters, and waitstaff. It is hoped the book will be appreciated by readers beyond the trade, including wine collectors, oenophiles, and the growing legion of the wine-obsessed or those curious about wine and how it can be best served.

Charlie Trotter believes that any restaurant can develop a top-flight wine program, regardless if the wine tab at the table is $30 or $300. Ingredients include choosing wines with care, serving them in attractive stemware, and training the service staff to work seamlessly with the kitchen to ensure that the food and the wine complement each other. Many argue that no restaurant in America does it better than Trotter's.

But the most critical element in crafting an exceptional wine program and the service that surrounds it is passion. And passion, says Trotter, doesn't cost a dime. In the pages that follow, Trotter and his wine team share lessons on extraordinary wine service.

1

Jazzin' It Up

Improvisational Wine-Food Pairings

A t Trotter's, a chef would never resist a request that a dish be adapted to a wine. The attitude, common to many kitchens, that "This is my dish! Nothing can change it. You must find the wine for the dish," doesn't wash in a restaurant where there's a critical synergy between the wine and the food.

"There's an unlimited number of ways a dish can be adjusted to a wine," Charlie Trotter says. "We can add acid or reduce the amount of acid; we can tweak the degree of earthy notes in a dish; or we could replace a primary ingredient of a dish by, for example, replacing a pigeon with a Dover sole. When the guest orders a certain wine, we can work the food around the wine."

Trotter says his kitchen's agility and flexibility with regard to the wine being poured in the dining room is unique: "There's no other restaurant that essentially says, 'Would you like to have this kind of food to fit the red wine you are drinking?' And we do that across four different menus a night—the grand, the vegetable, the raw, and the kitchen table."

As an example of how the tail sometimes wags the dog, Trotter described this scenario: A table orders a 1959 Château Margaux, a first-growth from Bordeaux that's big and bold. It's an expensive bottle. But the first course on the menu is raw *hamachi* with lemongrass juice. There's little harmony between a full-bodied red wine and raw fish. The sommelier alerts the kitchen, which adapts on the fly by changing the flavor profile to match the wine. A quail leg confit with droplets of black truffle juice is brought to the table to better harmonize with the wine.

The kitchen is expected to make those types of in-the-moment accommodations throughout the evening. "We are always adjusting the flavor profile of a dish to match the wine," Trotter says. "I'm not concerned with how that makes things for the kitchen. Everything we do is considered à la minute, made to order. For example, we can take a piece of raw codfish and braise it with red wine and mushrooms and also prepare something on the side that was not part of the original dish to better accommodate a red wine a guest may have ordered. That's the beauty of this. We can be spontaneous."

LIKE A ROLLING STONE

Trotter says he learned a great deal about the interplay between wine and food from Larry Stone in the early days of the restaurant. "I was no wine expert, but I understood the basics of acid and floral notes and tannins and the concentrations of fruit within the wines, and I would try to organize ideas around that. But Larry helped me bring my understanding to a different level. He would come to the kitchen and whisper in my ear that a guest had ordered a 1970 Château Petrus and could I sauce the dish with more acidic notes. It was that kind of interplay, like Mick Jagger and Keith Richards or Michael Jordan and Scotty Pippen. They had their roles and they would play off each other, and one could not necessarily succeed without the other."

Trotter concedes that he and Stone, whose food knowledge he greatly respected, did not always see eye to eye on the pairings. "We had a few friendly spats in the kitchen over the years, and that's healthy because we almost always arrived at a pairing that worked. He was always about delivering the best possible product and service to the table. He was simply the best at wine and food pairings.

"Larry Stone and I worked together like no other chef and sommelier did at the time. These days that kind of relationship is more common, but not at that time. It was unheard of, because most chefs would overrule the sommelier by saying that they would not make the accommodations to suit the wine. A chef would never hear of it and would simply tell the sommelier to find the right wine for the dish, not the other way around."

Food pairings, like everything else at Trotter's, don't adhere to a rule book. There is no book of rules. Trotter wouldn't hear of it. But that's not to say there aren't some basic guidelines. One of the most important considerations is the level of acidity in a dish. If it's high in acid, the sommelier may complement it with a wine that has tart overtones, such as Champagne, Pinot Blanc, or chardonnay.

Or the wine can contrast with the dish. A sweet wine like a Riesling can offset the spicy heat of barbecue or an Asian preparation. Dessert wines invariably need to be sweeter than what the pastry chef has put on the plate, red wine still pairs with red meat, and white wine is a reliable companion to fish and poultry. Other considerations influencing a pairing include the texture of the dish, its cooking method, and how it is sauced. At Trotter's, where the chefs and the sommeliers possess highly sophisticated palates, just

> "Trotter has created a unique synergy with the food and the wine. He recognizes that the wine is fixed, whereas the food is variable. He will downplay a flavor or tweak an ingredient to enhance the wine-food pairing."
>
> —Evan Goldstein, Master Sommelier and author of *Perfect Pairings: A Master Sommelier's Practical Advice for Partnering Wine with Food*

about any combination of food and wine is likely to end up at the table. So long as it works, of course. (See the Appendix for more pairing examples.)

ADOPTING A CHEF'S MINDSET

Trotter's longtime chef de cuisine Matthias Merges says the best sommeliers are the ones with the sensibilities of a good chef. "A good sommelier not only has to know wine and the provenance of the wine, but he or she must have a great palate for food and truly appreciate it. What we try to get across here is the seamlessness between the food and the wine. For us in the kitchen, we treat wine like food. Just as we taste the food and explore all its components, we taste the wine, looking for balance, the structure, and the different notes. That is how you learn to pair food and wine."

There's no hostility or distrust between the chef and the sommelier, says Merges. "The sommeliers have come into the kitchen with challenging, even what seems to us to be absurd, requests, but their requests are always honored. In many restaurants, the food and the wine are completely separate. The food is the food and it will never change, regardless of the wine being served at the table. But here, it's just the opposite.

"If a guest asks us to create a menu around the wine, we have the ability to change all the details in the food to match the wine. The wine is constant, the food is malleable. We are much more spontaneous in our kitchen, and we can use that to our advantage. We have many more opportunities each night to match the wine and play up or play down certain notes in the food."

> "The stories of Trotter changing dishes on the fly to accommodate the wine are legendary. Some people think it's a stunt. But he doesn't hesitate to alter a dish or to open a bottle that is appropriate."
>
> —William Rice, former food and wine writer for the *Chicago Tribune*

PREMIUM WINE EXPERIENCE

Introduced shortly before the restaurant's twentieth anniversary celebration in 2007, the Premium Wine Experience was designed for guests seeking a unique tasting experience.

A number of guests who had enjoyed the Wine Accompaniment (see page 19) indicated they would be willing to pay for a pairing of the food with some of the world's most classic wines, Trotter says. "For a party of four, for example, it would require opening five or six bottles of super-premium wine to cover each course, but the cost would become prohibitive."

Inspired by the Wine Accompaniment concept, Trotter's developed—over the course of a year of research, testing, and staff training—a by-the-glass Premium Wine Experience that complements the evening's food courses. À la the Wine Accompaniment, sommeliers pour two and a half ounces—or a half-glass—of wine for each course of the Premium Wine Experience. About 10 percent of the guests each evening opt for the Premium Wine Experience.

The cost is $250, which is in addition to the price of the meal. Not easy to swallow for diners on a budget—yet if they were individually to buy a bottle of each item on the Premium Wine Experience, they might pay more than $2,000. The wines in the program had not been previously available by the glass. Pouring glasses from those ultra-premium wines is a risk for Trotter's because what remains in the bottle usually can't be sold. But it doesn't go to waste, because the restaurant will, for example, bring a glass or glasses of the wine to the table of a visiting chef or a culinary student or a special friend of the house. The complimentary glass will often be accompanied by an extra food course matched to the wine. Although the bottle may represent a loss or a substantially reduced margin, it's more than recouped with the goodwill it has generated.

"The Premium Wine Experience is a different kind of journey that pairs world-class wines from France, Germany, and Italy, as well as some New World wines that have established themselves as benchmarks, with our cuisine," Reddick explains. "The guest can experience some of the most prized, most luxurious wines from our list without having to commit to a single bottle, which could be as much as $1,000."

Here is the introductory Premium Wine Experience list:

Krug "Grand Cuvee" Brut MV

Benedict Loosen-Erben "Urziger Wurzgarten" Riesling Spätlese, Mosel 1991

Kistler "Vine Hill" Russian River 2003

Nuits-Saint-Georges "Les Vaucrains" Nicolas Potel 1998

Henschke "Hill of Grace" Shiraz, South Australia 1992

Kracher "No. 1-Zwischen den Seen" Zweigelt Trockenbeerenauslese, Burgenland 1998

Warre's Vintage Port 1977

IN THE MOMENT

In the broadest of terms, the degustation menus at Trotter's progress from lighter fare to darker, more full-bodied fare. White wines work better than reds at the outset of the progression. But guests with a preference for red wine may forgo a white wine, which would seem to frustrate efforts for an evening of sensible pairings. A member of the wine service team will alert the kitchen, and the kitchen will often send the wine service team member back to the table to gather more information from the guests about their tastes. A member of the kitchen staff may even join the conversation at tableside.

"The sommelier or I might say: 'We've noticed you have ordered this type of wine. Would you like us to tailor the menu around the wine?' If the answer is yes, the guests have put themselves in our hands with the expectation that we are going to create a dining experience that matches the food to the wine."

Merges uses the example of a guest who orders a 1997 Araujo cabernet sauvignon, which he describes as "big and delicious." He says from the *amuse* course at the start to the dessert course at the finish, the kitchen will build a menu with the wine in mind.

The sommelier's role is critical, and he or she is expected to carefully and insightfully collect intelligence for the kitchen throughout the evening. For example, the sommelier might tip off the kitchen that the guests at a certain table have more than half a bottle of red wine left at the table, but it's time to move on to another course. Merges says he might add a course to pair with the remaining bottle of red to better orchestrate the dining experience. It wouldn't make sense to begin preparing dessert when there's half a bottle of red wine at the table.

"It's important for us to know how each table is doing and how the energy in the entire restaurant feels," Merges says. "We're often looking for very specific information from the sommelier. We're constantly communicating with them about the pairings. The sommelier will sometimes bring a small sample of the wine being poured at the table into the kitchen, and we'll taste it on the fly. That might influence how we sauce the dish. We're working very spontaneously. Nothing is set until the dish is delivered to the table. That's what we teach here: anything can change at any moment."

"Trotter's is an environment where the wine and the food have been partnered at a very sophisticated, complex level. Wine is a fundamental contributor to his development as a chef and his success as a restaurateur."

—Thomas Matthews, executive editor of *Wine Spectator*

THE SCIENCE OF SERENDIPITY

Larry Stone recalls how the kitchen at Trotter's was a bit like a fast-paced laboratory each night, with wine and food tastings and pairings conducted on a moment's notice in order to deliver an unforgettable dining experience to the guest. It was not for the faint of heart, because both the kitchen staff and the wine service team had to be able to turn on a dime.

On weekend evenings, when the restaurant is serving upwards of 190 guests a night, the kitchen operates at a frenetic pace. On nights like that, a sommelier needs to be tactful about his or her on-the-fly requests that a chef adjust a dish or do something extra-ordinary for the sake of the wine, says sommelier Conrad Reddick. "I might stop in the kitchen and ask if we could do something special for a table that just ordered this great bottle of white Burgundy. We were planning to do a red wine course, but that's now changed. I'll ask the chef if there's any way we could do a special course with a roasted rabbit with squash purée and carrots. That would be much friendlier to the white Burgundy."

"Trotter could not have been as successful as he has been, or advanced his cuisine to the level it is, without emphasizing the wine."

— Thomas Matthews, executive editor of *Wine Spectator*

To ensure that his suggestion doesn't fall on deaf ears, Reddick is careful to phrase it as a request rather than a demand. He'll cajole them with a nice word about the magnificent cuisine the kitchen is producing and how well it's being received in the dining room. He might even offer additional tidbits of intelligence from the dining room by studying the tickets at the expediter's station and explaining that guests from one of those tables have struck up a conversation with guests from a neighboring table.

Guest-to-guest interplay is hardly discouraged, but it often slows the dining pace. "So I'll mention that and suggest the chef drop table number three back a fire because the table will not be ready for that course," Reddick says. Offerings like that are much appreciated by the kitchen, which will show its appreciation by accommodating the sommelier's request, underscoring the notion that you can catch more flies with honey than with vinegar.

A SNEAK PREVIEW

Sommelier Molly Wismier says she spends time talking to the chefs prior to service so she fully understands what's on the menu that night. Her preservice conversation might focus on what flavors in a dish they are planning to emphasize, which could influence her selection or recommendation of a wine. She'll discuss possible pairings that night that are more historical or classical as well as those that might be based on seasonal foodstuffs on the evening's menu. Ultimately, she has to make the right call on a pairing, which is strengthened by the amount of information she can glean beforehand from the kitchen.

The strong relationship between her and the kitchen pays dividends during the heat of battle. For example, she might notice that a guest doesn't like a certain dish. A telltale sign: the guest pushes the food around her plate with her fork but doesn't continue to eat it. Wismier will confirm her hunch by asking if the dish is to the guest's liking, or she may simply ask the kitchen to produce another dish.

The critical relationship between the sommelier and the chef relies heavily on mutual respect for each other. That can only be achieved through constant communication between the two before, during, and after service. The expediter, typically a senior person who serves as the liaison between the kitchen and the front-of-the-house staff and who controls the pace of service, needs to be sure that the sommelier and the chef are communicating clearly and respectfully throughout the evening. If the expediter becomes aware of a disconnection between the two key players, he needs to step in and get them back in sync. Often the chef de cuisine also serves as the expediter.

A sudden change of course may also precipitate a change in the wine selection. But when the chefs and the sommeliers have an open channel of communication, the process of providing the guest with an enjoyable dining experience is relatively seamless.

Trotter says top leaders at restaurants need to pay careful attention to the working relationship between key players such as the sommelier and chef de cuisine. A disconnect between the two can quickly become self-destructive and demoralize the staff. Service will suffer. Savvy leaders will call a meeting or series of meetings to resolve the differences between them.

RUBBING ELBOWS WITH THE GIANTS

Right from the start, Trotter began associating himself and his restaurant with some of the best winemakers in the world. He's done the same with the world's great chefs. Often he will invite both a leading winemaker and a prominent chef to be the stars of a special event at the restaurant, as he did in 2004 when he invited David Powell of Torbreck Vintners of Australia's Barossa Valley to pour his wine for a meal prepared by Chef Sergi Arola of Spain.

The events raised money for Charlie Trotter's Educational Foundation, which has collected more than $1 million for culinary education. Many of the scholarships have been awarded to students lacking the financial means to afford a culinary education.

Trotter estimates that over the years, fifty of the top winemakers in America have poured their wines at his restaurant. The visiting vintners read like a Who's Who: the late Andre Tchelistcheff, considered the dean of American winemakers; Mike Grgich, another Napa Valley legend and founder of Grgich Hills Cellar; and Warren Winiarski, founder of Stag's Leap Wine Cellars. The first winemaker featured at an event at Trotter's was Randall Grahm, the maverick president of Bonny Doon Vineyard in Santa Cruz, California. In a full-circle moment, the ever-provocative Grahm was among the winemakers who appeared at one of Trotter's twentieth-anniversary celebrations in October 2007.

The leading European winemakers were never reluctant to visit either. They were intrigued and flattered that an American chef was so devoted to their craft that he would build the menu around their product.

The restaurant's frequent hosting of the leading lights of food and wine underscored the importance of the impromptu interplay between wine and food. It was not lost on the staff, who relished the opportunity to rub elbows with the biggest names in the business.

"The staff knows that every couple of months they are going to encounter another great winemaker and another great chef, often in combination and often with multiple winemakers and multiple chefs," Trotter says. "It's unprecedented what we do here. Imagine having Richard Geoffrey, the winemaker from Dom Pérignon, come here to pour his wine and be joined by Tetsuya Wakuda of Sydney, Heston Blumenthal of London, and Pierre Hermé of Paris—three of the greatest chefs in the world—all here at the same time for an event. That's how seriously we take food and wine."

Visits from the industry's leading authorities motivate the staff to play to their level, and it reminds them that they are working at a place that matters. Trotter says restaurateurs shouldn't hesitate to invite a top name in food and wine to star at a special event at the restaurant. He extended invitations to the big names in the industry from the earliest days of the restaurant, and he admits he was surprised by how many of them accepted. The benefits of hosting a VIP far outweigh the costs of bringing him or her to the restaurant.

PRENUPTIAL AGREEMENTS

Wine and food pairings at Trotter's became more formalized in 2002 when the restaurant introduced its Wine Accompaniment program that matches the grand and vegetable tasting menus with a series of wines by the glass. It was more evolutionary than revolutionary because Trotter's has long accommodated guests who wanted a dish-by-dish wine pairing. Trotter disagrees with those who say the Wine Accompaniment robs the restaurant of some of its spontaneity, because the program exposes the guest to such a wide spectrum of the world's wine offerings. And the accompaniment is not set in stone. Accommodations can be made.

The $100 Wine Accompaniment menu showcases the work of small-production, artisanal wine growers from traditional regions as well as wine from up-and-coming regions such as New Zealand or Chile. Some are biodynamically produced. Although they are world-class in character, most of the wines have yet to achieve the kind of recognition enjoyed by the more classic selections.

WE ARE IN YOUR HANDS

About a third of the guests on any given evening opt for the Wine Accompaniment. Two to three ounces of each wine is poured into a guest's glass to accent each dish on the menu. "We have always had an extensive and eclectic wine-by-the-glass program," Trotter says. "But a glass-by-glass, dish-by-dish selection across seven or eight courses can become a bit overwhelming. Many of our guests over the years have been more than happy to let us make the selections for them. They wanted to put themselves in our hands and release themselves to the experience. They recognize us as the experts: 'Please select the wine and food for us.' But it's an enormous responsibility for us because our guests are paying a lot of money for what's to be an exquisite evening of wine and food."

The kitchen and wine service teams work closely together to orchestrate the pairings. Weekly wine and food tastings between the staffs allow them to marry the menus to the Wine Accompaniment, although informal conversations about pairing possibilities as well as impromptu tastings take place almost daily.

"A sommelier, for example, will tell me that we have this great Santiago Ruiz from Spain in the cellar, and ask, 'Would you consider building a dish around it?' And we'll do that with fennel and curry, accenting the herbaceous notes. The sommelier may tell us that a particular wine in our cellar is drinking beautifully right now and this would be the perfect time to build a dish around it. And we will do that.

"The spontaneity of the food and wine pairings at Trotter's makes it exciting ... even a little bit dangerous, because they are always right there on the edge establishing new standards."

—Thomas Keller, chef-owner of The French Laundry and Per Se

"On the other side of the coin, we might develop a dish and say to the sommelier that the ingredients are now in season and challenge him to find a great wine to go with it. We'll often taste several wines with a dish before we narrow it down. Sometimes we may not even have the right wine in-house and we'll have to look outside for the right wine to go with that particular course," Merges explains.

Once the trial and error is complete, the pairing will be introduced anywhere from a couple of days to a week later. But it's a continuous, improvisational process at Trotter's because menus change nightly. Jazz musicians, after all, rarely play the same song the same way.

Guests at Trotter's can drink wine by the glass, by the bottle, or by the formal accompaniment. Regardless of the option, Trotter says guests can count on pairings that create a whole greater than the sum of its parts. "We have a vast repertoire of wine; some are classic, some are esoteric, some are quirky. It's an embarrassment of riches that gives us a wealth of opportunities to create just the right match."

SERVICE POINTS

To ensure that sommeliers and chefs orchestrate the best possible wine and food pairings, consider these service points:

- Chefs need to be flexible. Even the great chefs must be willing to compromise elements of their signature dishes to optimize a wine pairing. Chefs should be willing to make any accommodation for a guest so long as it's logistically and financially possible. Trotter's philosophy is to do whatever it takes to please a guest.

- A sommelier should be quick to alert the kitchen to a guest's preference or an unexpected change in direction at a table.

- A chef and a sommelier can help educate each other about their respective specialties. A good cook needs to be a sommelier in a chef's body, and vice versa.

- Wine should be treated as a food. It should be tasted and tested for balance, structure, and different notes. That is how to learn to pair wine and food.

- Hostility between the wine service team and the culinary staff must not be tolerated. Even seemingly absurd requests from the wine team should be accommodated. The sommelier, however, may need to temper a guest's request for something extraordinary by gently negotiating with him or her to make it more manageable for the kitchen.

- Sommeliers need to be the eyes and ears of the kitchen by collecting all available intelligence from the dining room.

■ Small tasting samples of a wine, when appropriate, can be brought to the kitchen to help the chefs calibrate their dishes with the wine. Wine-savvy guests sometimes ask that a small sample of the wine they are drinking be tasted by the chef.

■ A little tact and diplomacy on the part of the sommelier goes a long way on nights when the kitchen's intensity is especially high.

■ Sommeliers should spend time in the kitchen prior to service to learn as much as possible about new seasonal foodstuffs on hand and how they might affect the evening's pairings.

■ Wine and food pairings can be formalized with programs such as Trotter's Wine Accompaniment or the Premium Wine Experience.

■ The wine team and culinary staff can be inspired by special events at the restaurant featuring leading winemakers and chefs.

2

Establishing a Legacy of Superlative Wine Service

To work as a sommelier at Charlie Trotter's is to inherit the legacy of two of America's most renowned sommeliers—Larry Stone and Joe Spellman.

First Stone, then Spellman. Both renaissance men. Both Master Sommeliers. Stone was a Fulbright scholar who, in addition to being the first American to win the title of International Best Sommelier in French Wines and Spirits, remains the only American to have earned the title of French Maître Sommelier from the Union de la Sommellerie Française.

Spellman was a classics major at the University of Chicago, where he read literary works in their original Greek and Latin. In 1997, ten years after Stone won the French Sommelier competition in Paris, Spellman bested thirty-one other national winners in Paris to claim the title of the world's best sommelier in French wines and spirits. He also holds the distinction of Certified Wine Educator, which requires passing a rigorous test.

BIG SHOES TO FILL

Linda Violago, who worked several stints as a sommelier at Trotter's between 2002 and 2006, allows that it was intimidating stepping into the shoes of such wizards of wine. "I knew that I would somehow have to work harder than they did, to somehow meet the incredibly high standards for service they set when they were here. It's because of them that this restaurant has the reputation as one of the world's great wine and food destinations."

Trotter frequently reminds members of his wine service team, and those on the general service staff who aspire to it, of the restaurant's legacy of service excellence. "I have told them that this restaurant has had the greatest collection over the years of the best sommeliers in the country. We have managed to attract the kind of people who want to live up to that reputation. It's like donning the pinstripes of the New York Yankees. The players wearing that uniform understand the enormous expectations and the team's history of success.

"The list of sommeliers who have worked at Charlie Trotter's reads like the roster in a Hall of Fame. Trotter's has hired world-class sommeliers to assure that the restaurant operates at the highest possible level. It was one of the earliest of the great American restaurants to put such an emphasis on wine, its cellars, and its list."

—Thomas Matthews, executive editor of *Wine Spectator*

"I don't want anyone to underappreciate what has been accomplished here. We have worked hard to create a culture of excellence here, and that's been done by pointing to the incredible work of those whose shoulders we stand on today. The fact that the great chefs and sommeliers of the world come here for anniversaries or other events sends a signal to our staff that they are working in a special place."

The importance of upholding the restaurant's legacy and the need to take it to the next level is a message that Trotter personally conveys at leadership team and staff meetings. Trotter's leadership team, in turn, frequently reminds the staff of how high the bar has been set.

Violago—who was raised in Vancouver, British Columbia, and joined Trotter's after serving as a sommelier in Queensland, Australia—said Trotter's reputation for excellence is something that should never be taken for granted. She constantly reminded herself and her wine service team members that if they were to fall short of the standards set by Stone and Spellman and their successors they could jeopardize the restaurant's standing. One bad night and the damage is done.

During a preservice meeting one evening, she expressed disappointment with the caliber of wine and food service from the previous night. "I see a lot of new faces in this room tonight and I want to remind everyone that we need to be more careful. We need to be more focused," she said with a determined, almost harsh edge to her voice. The eyes of several in the room grew wide as the message was absorbed.

GENTLEMEN AND SCHOLARS

Careful, focused service was one of the many hallmarks established by Stone and Spellman. But it was much more than that. Stone and Spellman both possessed scholarly knowledge about wine. They both were adept at pairing wine with food, and they both had a knack for making people feel at ease through the lively art of conversation.

They had a sixth sense for being able to read the needs of the guests, and each possessed an exquisitely calibrated palate. Unlike sommeliers who only handle the wine, Stone and Spellman eagerly pitched in at every point of service—from greeting guests at the door to running and clearing food to pulling chairs at the table for customers. "Larry and Joe were never the kind of sommeliers who stood there with the tastevin around their neck offering sage advice about wine," Charlie Trotter says. "They were always willing to jump in at any point to be a part of service. They established a hands-on tradition that continues today."

They were anything but the stereotypical effete, haughty French sommeliers. Their style—and the style that persists at Trotter's today—was a blend of graciousness, modesty, and erudition while being technically precise. Stone was noted for his intensity and knowledge; Spellman for his more easygoing, everyman style. "Larry Stone was the sommelier's sommelier; Joe Spellman was the people's sommelier," Trotter says.

SHARING WISDOM AND EXPERIENCES

Both Spellman and Stone were known for carving out time amid their busy schedules to mentor and train junior members of the staff. That too is a tradition that lives on at Trotter's. Sommeliers are expected to share as much knowledge about wine and wine service as possible both during formal training sessions and during service on the dining room floor or in the cellars each evening. The training and mentoring is meant to challenge the more novice members of the wine service team.

Trotter's would have seemed an unlikely destination for Stone in 1989. By that stage of his career, he had already become a Master Sommelier and had been selected by an international jury as the number one sommelier in French wines and spirits. He was sent by the Four Seasons Hotels and Resorts to Chicago to develop its wine program there.

While in Chicago, Stone became a member of the fledgling Chicago Sommeliers Society founded by Charlie Trotter's then-wife, Lisa. The society was an opportunity for the growing sommelier community in Chicago to share the common experiences of their trade. Lisa began recruiting Stone to replace her as wine director and general manager at Trotter's, as she was planning to return to graduate school.

Although Trotter's gets deluged with job applications, Charlie Trotter says it's important for him and his leadership team to know the talent in a local or even national market so they will be prepared if and when an opening develops. The best restaurants have to actively recruit talent, and participating in the culinary community or in local trade associations allows restaurateurs to stay abreast of rising stars and be aware of their possible availability.

Trotter's, which launched to the tune of positive reviews, was only two years old at the time. Yet Stone says he didn't consider taking his considerable talents to Trotter's a bad bet, despite his position at the Four Seasons. "I didn't think I was taking a big risk. I knew that Trotter was a talented chef. The problem with a lot of great chefs is that they're convinced that their cuisine is so great that the wine is only incidental. That wasn't the case with Charlie. He has a unique appreciation for the food and wine combination. I knew that I had made the right move."

Despite having to endure several twenty-four-hour shifts and working his first months at Trotter's in a back brace because of a spinal cord injury, Stone says he did not experience much buyer's remorse, primarily because he was given such enormous latitude by Trotter to develop a world-class wine program.

CRAMPED AND CROWDED BEGINNINGS

But the early days had their challenges. He recalls a cramped wine cellar and overcrowded conditions on the weekends to make up for the lack of weeknight traffic. "I remember some frustration in the first three months because we were overbooked on the weekends. You could barely get out of the restaurant because of the crowds and some people would even have to wait outside. I told Charlie: 'What's the point of having irate customers? They're just going to walk out.' Things were a little loose in those days." Such was the price of a wildly popular restaurant.

The service problems were eventually ironed out, and Stone was able to concentrate on taking the wine program to the next level. He inherited an eight-page list with about 125 wines. "There were some nice choices; interesting wines from California and France, including several varietals from the Rhône Valley." He said the wines were relatively inexpensive, with some of the most expensive in the $50 to $60 range.

Stone began compiling an enhanced list, and one day he went to Trotter and his late father, Bob, whose support and financial backing helped launch the restaurant. Stone presented to Charlie and his father his recommendations totaling more than $35,000, including a small cache of Burgundies, which remain a mainstay of the list today. "I never expected Charlie and Bob would agree to it, because the restaurant was not yet profitable. But they did."

The wine list continued to grow after Trotter's purchased the cellar of Le Provencal, a restaurant in nearby Evanston with a wine inventory valued at about $250,000. The problem now was where to store the growing wine inventory. A new cellar was created on the second floor of the restaurant and some had to be stored off-site.

THE ARRIVAL OF THE OENOPHILE

As the list continued to grow, Stone felt more comfortable inviting wine-savvy guests to the restaurant. "I brought in a lot of wine people, but they were wary of Charlie because he was not considered a classic French chef. The gourmets of Chicago were uneasy with Charlie's flair for Italian and Asian food. They thought his food was too eccentric, too daring at the time, and many were convinced that you can't pair Asian food with Western wine."

But Stone relished the challenge of pairing his wine with Trotter's refined, focused food. "Charlie respected my food knowledge and he liked working with me on the food pairings. It was an exciting time for the restaurant. The kitchen was like a little laboratory every night. The guests were impressed with the pairings and would be tickled, for example, when a special sauce was prepared especially for a food and wine combination."

That style of spontaneous wine and food pairings in the spirit of the great jazz musicians like Miles Davis and John Coltrane came to amaze the guests and was incorporated into the restaurant's unwritten playbook.

PUTTING WINE ON A PEDESTAL

Another innovation introduced by Stone, which has become a tradition at Trotter's, is the marble-topped credenza used in each dining room to open and serve wine. The credenza became a staging area from which the wine service team members would open and taste the wine before it was served to the guest. "In those days, restaurants would say: 'Caveat emptor.' You buy the wine in our restaurant at your own risk. But Charlie wanted the highest possible operating standards to ensure the wine was right."

The sommelier would taste each bottle to ensure that it was not corked and that its taste was true. It was more than just quality control. The credenza provided a focal point for the wine service in each dining room, an altar on which the ritual was performed in full view of the guests. It added a flair to the wine service. The wine list had grown to about eight hundred selections. By the time Stone left in 1993 to return to the West Coast, he had made an indelible imprint on the restaurant and its wine service.

Lisa Trotter (now Lisa Ehrlich-Giglio) played a pivotal role in recruiting Joe Spellman to replace Stone. In fact, she had first tried to recruit Spellman as her replacement, but at the time he was wary of Trotter's ferocious reputation. Trotter was once voted the second-meanest Chicagoan by *Chicago* magazine. Michael Jordan was first. Trotter, who is better known in the culinary field these days for his philanthropy, is dismissive of the designation, although he didn't mind being mentioned in the same breath with Jordan—like himself, a man with a bent for perfection.

But when Stone left, Spellman decided it was time to go to work at Trotter's. And like Stone, Spellman had amassed an impressive resume, having been in charge of wine programs at such respected fine dining spots as the Pump Room, the Park Hyatt, and Maxim's. While studying at the University of Chicago, Spellman had tended bar at Mallory's, an upscale restaurant in the Hyde Park neighborhood near the University. After Spellman expressed a curiosity about wine, the owner treated him to a bottle of Puligny-Montrachet by Domaine Leflaive. From that point on, says Spellman, wine became the focal point of his career.

CHANGING OF THE GUARD

"It was quite a coup for Trotter's to land Larry Stone as its sommelier," says Spellman, who, despite his impressive resume, wasn't sure he could possibly do better than Stone in that role. But he figured the time was right, and he signed on with Trotter's. It was an especially dynamic time for the restaurant and its wine service. The menu was changing from à la carte to degustation, which would have huge implications for the wine list and wine service; the cellars were being expanded and reorganized; and the first in a large collection of Trotter's cookbooks was being written.

The books proved to be an opportunity for Spellman to work closely with the kitchen in preparing and tasting dishes to be paired with wines. "The cuisine and the wine became more complex; it required a great deal of attention. But the degustation menu allowed the guest to experience a wider range of foodstuffs available in the kitchen that evening, and it gave the wine team more of an opportunity to maximize the experience for the guest each night. It allowed us to help the guests explore parts of the wine world that were somewhat unexplored for them."

It was also a time when the restaurant invested heavily in Riedel, the Austrian glassware maker of 24 percent lead crystal stemware. The respect for the wine was also evident in the way a bottle of wine was handled in the restaurant. Spellman says it was always label up and cradled in a white tablecloth. The wine was treated reverently, regardless of whether guests were present.

> "Larry Stone and Joseph Spellman were absolutely brilliant. They could ante up to anything in the Paris sommelier competition."
>
> —William Rice, former food and wine writer for the *Chicago Tribune*

More gregarious than his predecessor, Spellman reveled in his time at tableside, but had no qualms about playing any of the less glamorous roles at the restaurant, such as running food from the kitchen or pitching in to wash dishes. "I respected every single aspect of the restaurant's operation in order to make a great evening for the guest. My goal was always to take care of people, making sure they felt they were getting a good value so they could revel in the dining experience."

CROWNING A NEW MASTER

Unlike Stone, who arrived at Trotter's with his Master Sommelier designation in hand, Spellman had to study for his MS exam while working the long hours at Trotter's. Married with children, Spellman spent many mornings preparing for the notoriously difficult three-part exam. He failed all three parts on his first try in 1995, but passed in 1997, becoming the second Master Sommelier to ply the dining rooms at Trotter's. Currently the winery sommelier for Justin Vineyards & Winery in Paso Robles, California, Spellman is also chair of the American Chapter of the Court of Master Sommeliers.

He hasn't lost his ability to spin a good yarn. At the Master Sommeliers' dinner in San Francisco honoring his former boss, he rose to sing Trotter's praises. Well, sort of. He described how he encountered Trotter in an empty dining room late one night after a charity event in the restaurant to raise money for victims of the 1993 floods that ravaged communities along the Mississippi River.

Having just started at Trotter's and having yet to establish a rapport with Trotter, Spellman opted for a little small talk. "Well that was fun!" Spellman chirped innocently. "Fun?!" barked Trotter in response. "It's not about having fun. It's about excellence!"

Spellman's story brought down the house, including Trotter, who's well aware of how hard he pushes his team. But that's life with Charlie, who has never tolerated anything less than a person's best and most sincere effort.

THE GENESIS OF THE PROGRAM

Spellman and Stone credit Ehrlich-Giglio for launching the restaurant's wine program on the right foot as its first wine buyer and sommelier. To prepare for a French bistro they envisioned opening one day in Chicago, Lisa and Charlie traveled throughout Europe, primarily France, to dine in some of its best restaurants, including Girardet, the kitchen of the great Frédy Girardet, and L'Auberge du Pont de Collonges, where renowned chef Paul Bocuse holds court.

The dining experiences inspired them as they began a catering business in Chicago, the precursor to the restaurant they opened in August 1987. "We did dozens of dinners in people's homes to create the kind of experience we wanted diners to experience in our restaurant." Charlie, of course, was the chef, while Lisa would manage the dining room. But she also wanted to buy and steward the wine. She got her wish and pieced together a wine cellar valued at about $30,000. (Fast forward twenty years and you'll find single bottles in the cellar worth more than the entire inventory of 1987.)

But Lisa made the most of a limited inventory that included varietals from Burgundy, the Loire Valley, and the Rhône Valley. Within the first six months, the restaurant was garnering glowing reviews for its innovative cuisine and wines to match. "Trotter's became a wine destination very quickly. I was less interested in the wine's pedigree. I was more interested in wines that enhanced the dining experience," she says. "We were one of the first restaurants to experiment with a vast array of wines by the glass. And we usually had a story about the wine that made the dining experience more personal for the guest."

Lisa made the best use of her intuitive powers at tableside to divine the wine preferences of her guests, which is the practice today. "You really need to be a good psychologist as you try to draw them out about what they like to drink, what they've enjoyed before. It's also important to know about the nature of their evening at the restaurant. Is it a celebration or is it to be a quiet romantic evening where they would prefer only a few interruptions? On the other hand, some guests would want all sorts of information about the wine—from the vinification process to the background of the winery founder."

She said her immediate successors—Stone and Spellman—were masters at intuiting the needs of their guests based on the conversations they had with them.

In many cases, the service staff knows the nature of the guests' evening. People making reservations are quick to share that they are celebrating an anniversary or a birthday. Guests figure they'll be treated with extra flair that evening. The reservationists are encouraged to collect as much information as the guests are willing to divulge. That information is noted in the restaurant's electronic database that is reviewed by the staff prior to service. Returning guests are always noted.

But some guests are not as forthcoming. In that case, the sommelier or other members of the service may subtly try to learn what's brought them to the restaurant that evening. Sommelier Conrad Reddick uses a range of techniques. "I may go right to the table and ask them directly: 'Are you celebrating something tonight or are you here just to have dinner?' Sometimes, I play more the role of detective. I might overhear the guests mention to someone at another table that they are celebrating an anniversary. Or I might seize on certain words I pick up in conversation with them to learn more about why they are here. Knowing why can be enormously helpful in making a pleasant evening for them."

PAYING TRIBUTE

Serafin Alvarado, who earned his MS while working at Trotter's, flew in from Chicago to toast his former boss that evening at Rubicon in San Francisco. "The kitchen at Trotter's has great respect for wine," Alvarado says, noting that the wine-centric mindset pervades the restaurant. "It's a vastly different sensibility, and it's reflected in how he trains people, how he stores the wine, how he buys the glassware, and how he writes the list."

One of the most important skills he learned at Trotter's was how to master the tableside conversation, in which a productive discussion often focuses on what the guests have liked or disliked in the past. Armed with the information, Alvarado could make a recommendation that "blows the table away. With about 1,600 wine selections at the time, we had a lot of tools to work with."

A CASE OF THE JITTERS

Discerning a guest's tastes in wine is one of the most challenging experiences, yet the most rewarding, according to Alvarado, who was intimidated by the standards he was expected to uphold or surpass as a sommelier at Trotter's. "I felt the pressure here because it's a famous wine destination where people like Larry Stone and Joe Spellman have held the job before me. I remember my first night working the floor as a floating sommelier and one of the servers came up to me and said that the guests at table 22 wanted to speak to the sommelier. I was so nervous I was almost shaking."

Alvarado shook off the jitters with each passing night on the floor as he grew into a role he had long dreamed about. "I knew this was my big chance, and I was going to make the most of it." Alvarado developed an interest in wine while working part-time in a restaurant as he earned his degree in chemistry at the University of Puerto Rico. He then worked at a restaurant in Ponce, Puerto Rico, that had a small wine program; there he worked his way up to sommelier.

"It was there that I became aware of Charlie Trotter's and I began buying his books. I was fascinated with a line from him about following your passion. I decided that if I was to be truly passionate about my job that I would have to do it at the highest possible level."

He wrote Trotter a letter explaining how he'd been inspired by him and how he believed he was ready to work in his restaurant's wine program. There was no response. The restaurant gets thousands of letters from job applicants every year. But one day, long after Alvarado figured his correspondence had ended up in the dead letter file, Trotter called and said he had an opening on his service staff. Alvarado vividly recalled the brief phone conversation. It was on a Wednesday; Trotter wanted to talk to him on Friday.

A FATEFUL ENCOUNTER

He flew to Chicago, where he met with Trotter and shadowed the wine team during two nights of service. It confirmed his sense that he wanted to work toward becoming a sommelier at Trotter's. Before he left, Trotter gave him his book *Lessons in Excellence from*

Charlie Trotter (Ten Speed Press, 1999) and told him they would talk after the holidays. An offer was extended and Alvarado joined the restaurant.

He was essentially starting over, because for the next nine months he was running food, clearing tables, and escorting guests to their table. But he was learning the inner workings of the restaurant, which is key to being a sommelier at Trotter's—the person in that position requires a sixth sense for everything that transpires during the evening in the restaurant.

Alvarado says he was not the least bit discouraged by his nine months of boot camp at Trotter's. "It was a test of my commitment, but I was psyched. I was getting a feel for the whole operation, and I knew that down the line it would only make me stronger as a sommelier."

"Charlie Trotter's has attracted some of the best sommeliers in America. What's especially impressive is that so many of them have gone on to enjoy success in other restaurants and other ventures after they have left Trotter's. They have all been wonderful role models for the younger or the newer members of the staff."

—Thomas Keller, chef-owner of The French Laundry and Per Se

Graceful and outgoing, Alvarado went on to become one of the best. Like Spellman, he earned his MS while working nights at Trotter's and studying by day for the three-part MS exam. Each night on the floor at Trotter's was an invaluable practicum for the service component of the MS exam. Trotter is proud of how well his people do on the service part of the exam, thanks to their solid grounding in all the details of properly and passionately caring for a guest.

Alvarado, who now works as a wine educator for Southern Wine and Spirits, says he was struck by the level of commitment required to excel night after night in a dining room with smart, sometimes demanding guests. "I had to be on my game technically, physically, and psychologically. Succeeding in any field requires incredible energy and dedication. If I only wanted to be comfortable, I would have never come to Trotter's because you need so much passion and stamina to succeed. Trotter always pushed me to the next level to see if I could succeed."

Despite the pressure of high expectations, Alvarado found the experience gratifying. "Once you have the knowledge and the confidence and all the other pieces come together, you start having fun. The best part is being able to see the reaction of a guest who's instantly blown away by the wine you just poured. It's also great to be able to work with some of the best wine and food in the world."

TRAFFICKING IN TROPHY WINES

Former Trotter's sommelier Robert Houde says one of the joys of wine service at the restaurant was that the wines were not there for their trophy value, as is the case in some fine-dining establishments. "At Trotter's, you actually got to work with the wine on the list. I pulled a lot of great wines from a list that grew from about 1,000 selections to more than 1,500 in the years I was there."

Delivering $1,500 bottles of wine to tables was not unusual on any given evening. Knowing that he had an impressive repertoire of selections at his disposal, Houde says he could confidently challenge guests at a table by offering to take them to a region they might not have explored or exposing them to an unfamiliar varietal. "We got the chance at every table to take people where they had never been before. People enjoy being surprised."

Some guests might take a quick look at the then-thirty-two-page list and slam it shut before asking, with a hint of desperation, "What should I do?" Houde saw that as the perfect opportunity to allay the guest's anxiety by striking up a conversation about some of their previous experiences with wine, gently probing to determine what might work.

"Some people would come in and say, 'We can only afford a $50 bottle of wine.' I'd say: 'Great. I will blow you away!'" Houde relished the challenges that nearly every table presented. "Working there was like being in a completely different universe," says Houde, now the general manager of Garnacha Ltd., a distributor of fine estate wines from Spain. "The list had such enormous breadth. It wasn't just a French list, but a global list."

Houde estimates that in his first three months of working on the wine service team at Trotter's his wine knowledge increased about 300 percent. "Not only are you surrounded by great wine, but you are tasting it every day, describing it and studying it." Of course, the expectations for the quality of the wine service were extremely high. "But helping you meet those expectations is the great product and a great staff to work with. There were no boundaries."

TAKING A DETOUR FROM THE KITCHEN

Jason Smith enrolled in the Culinary Institute of America in Hyde Park, New York, to prepare for a career in the kitchen. But after taking the standard six-week sequence in wine at the CIA, Smith was smitten. On graduating from the prestigious culinary college, Smith first took a job in a wine shop and later one in the cellar at the 21 Club in New York City before landing a spot on the service team at Trotter's in 2000. His goal was to become a sommelier.

He spent several months working the front door and running food before earning a spot as a server. He also began playing a role on the wine service team, where his knowledge of food and how it partners with wine was an obvious advantage. Focused and serious-minded, Smith achieved his goal of becoming a sommelier at Trotter's, which he realized was just another term for the best service person in the restaurant.

"You can't stand off in a corner of the dining room and turn your nose up and only step up when wine needs to be described or poured, like some sommeliers. Being a sommelier at Trotter's means you do everything for the guest, but that makes you a better team member. That's important because your team members can also help you at every turn and that makes you a better sommelier."

Smith, who in 2006 became Master Sommelier at Michael Mina at Bellagio in Las Vegas, credits Charlie Trotter for instilling in him a tireless work ethic. "He made it clear that he expected a great deal out of me. But I wanted to do more than meet his expectations. I wanted to exceed them."

SCULPTING A LIST

Charlie Trotter says you don't need a $2 million wine inventory or nearly two thousand different selections in the cellar to craft a brilliant wine list. What is paramount is creativity and the willingness to take a few risks. Look for quality wines from less-celebrated wine growing regions and from producers who have yet to make the A-list, but who are on their way. Prices will be more manageable, and guests will appreciate getting in on the ground floor of the next big thing in wine. Writing smart, creative lists requires lots of research, which for most wine aficionados is a labor of love. Lists are typically based on varietals or regions. "But there are many ways you can differentiate your list. It speaks to your restaurant's imagination," Trotter says. "You can build your wine list around courses. For example, you could build your list around wines that go great with steak or those that pair nicely with shellfish."

IN SEARCH OF PERFECTION

The expectations were enormous—not just from Trotter, but also from the guests themselves. "They come to Trotter's expecting perfection and you want to deliver on their expectations. It was understood that we would take ownership of the guest's experience because we were given 100 percent discretion to do whatever was necessary. In the event we hit a bump in the road, a sommelier had a variety of options to turn things around. If something unfortunate happened, you could do something positive to turn the mistake into a positive experience for the guest," says Smith.

The restaurant's tradition of excellence in wine service and its blue-chip wine list could sometimes weigh heavily on Smith. "It started with Lisa, then Larry, then Joe, and the other great sommeliers who worked there. Each of them managed to push the quality of the service and the quality of the list forward. I had this incredible sense of responsibility and duty. I didn't want to let any of them down. It's a legacy that can be hard to live up to. I sometimes go online and marvel at the list to see what has been added."

Smith handled his responsibilities well, all the while studying to become a Master Sommelier. With Trotter's usual support and encouragement, Smith completed his Advanced Sommelier coursework offered by the Court of Master Sommeliers while at Trotter's. It wasn't until his second try that he earned his MS, in 2005, after he had left Trotter's. His strong suit was the service component of the exam, in which all Trotter-trained candidates excel.

Smith noted that the demanding service atmosphere simulated by the Court of Master Sommeliers examiners was remarkably similar to what he had experienced countless evenings on the floor at Trotter's. Naturally, he felt fairly comfortable going through his paces under the examiners' scrutiny.

Reflecting on his three-and-a-half-year stint at Trotter's, Smith said one of the great rewards was the opportunity to work with sophisticated, appreciative guests, who on any given evening might have flown in from other parts of the country to wine and dine at Trotter's. Even better was the support Trotter provided his sommeliers. "The bottles he allowed us to open and taste were amazing," Smith says. "He was very generous with the wine and his support of the Court of Master Sommeliers program. It was clear the wine program and the people on the team were a priority."

SERVICE POINTS

Trotter's distinguished cast of former sommeliers share a wealth of ideas on how they added value to the wine service. Consider the following service points:

- A restaurant with a distinguished past should make its history a point of motivation for the staff, who may be inspired to maintain or improve on the standards of their predecessors.

- A sommelier must master the art of conversation to put the guests at ease and effectively collect information from them that will inform the food and wine pairings. Some sommeliers are naturally charismatic. Those who are not need to concentrate on becoming superb listeners and to be alert for clues as to what the guest truly wants. Tableside skills can be enhanced through training, observation, and experience.

- Sommeliers should never be aloof from general service. They should pitch in on the seemingly mundane matters in the dining room by pulling chairs, not just corks.

- Owners and managers should take the time to mentor and train newer members of the staff, by arranging impromptu wine tastings or pulling them aside to reflect on a service error or a job well done.

- Newer restaurants should take some risks with their wine lists.

- Wine service is elevated by the creation of a centerpiece for wine service in a dining room, such as the credenza introduced by sommelier Larry Stone. This allows the guests to focus their attention on some of the service's elegant rituals.

- Each wine should be tasted before it is served to a guest, to be certain that its taste is true and that it is not faulted. This quality control measure has spared Trotter's embarrassment and enhanced the reputation of its wine program.

- When the menu is expanded or altered the wine list should also be updated. It's important that the two evolve together.

- It is helpful to visit and study other restaurants with distinguished reputations as potential role models for your own restaurant or start-up.

- Staff must understand the nature of a guest's evening in the restaurant. For example, guests sharing a romantic dinner may require a level of attention different from what the staff would provide to guests who are dining to talk business.

- Sommeliers should not hesitate to share positive feedback from guests about a dish that had been altered to better suit the wine.

- Sommeliers must master every service role in the front of the house to truly understand the rhythm of the restaurant.

- Sommeliers, who are vested with unlimited discretion, must take ownership of a guest's evening, along with other members of the service team and the kitchen, to ensure that it is a transcendent experience.

3

Hiring and Honing
Masters of Wine Service

Charlie Trotter's fields thousands of applications a year from people who want to cook or serve food and pour wine in the shrine to food and wine. From the blizzard of applications, Trotter and his senior managers cull candidates who they hope will become the next Larry Stone or Serafin Alvarado.

Trotter's hiring practices are unconventional. He has hired people with many years of restaurant experience, and he has tapped some with almost none. He has hired people from other fine dining establishments, and he has offered jobs to people who have worked in more casual dining environments such as steakhouses or resorts.

In the job interview, Trotter looks for a certain spark—some indication that the candidate is naturally endowed with such soft skills as enthusiasm, intuition, empathy, humility, and graciousness. Those qualities, essential for exceptional customer service, are impossible to teach, he believes. So it's critical that he recognize those skills in a candidate. He estimates he makes the right hiring choice about three-quarters of the time.

Once hired, the candidate will be intensively trained, mentored, and motivated. The educational process is so comprehensive that Trotter says it's the equivalent of an MBA for the hospitality industry. He's especially proud of his many graduates—consummate professionals—who have gone on to big things in other restaurants and other businesses.

THAT'S NOT MY DEPARTMENT

Trotter regards it as a bad sign when a new hire says he or she only wants to serve wine. In fact, he's had a few promising candidates bent on becoming sommeliers who balked at the prospect of spending one to two years working their way up the ranks. He doesn't want any prima donnas on his team. He looks for team players with a service mindset who are willing to play any role at the restaurant at just about any time.

Trotter forewarns candidates that the perceived glamour of working as a member of one of the world's most renowned wine and food service teams is overstated. The work is tough, and he and his team leaders demand excellence at every turn. He often paints the darkest possible picture of life at the restaurant. Candidates typically spend a couple of nights observing service, which he says only further motivates a serious candidate. The weaker or less sincere candidates realize the fast-paced precision of the restaurant is probably not for them.

"The dues-paying is a positive experience. Many people actually look forward to matriculating through the system," Trotter says. "They have a comprehensive understanding of how the restaurant operates by the time they're ready to describe and pour wine."

In this chapter, we will take an inside look at the various training and educational techniques that Trotter's employs to create a world-class wine service team. Trotter says training is perpetual. It comes in a variety of forms—ranging from a dry lecture on the provenance of a wine held in the dining room-turned-classroom to trips to many different wine-growing regions where his sommeliers meet winemakers and visit their vineyards.

Trotter—who is known to cast a penetrating stare in the direction of a staffer he's observed falling short of his famously high standards—says training is designed to educate and to motivate. "The more employees know about what's being done at the restaurant, the more excited about their jobs they will become," he says. Some of the training is more informal: a senior staffer or Trotter himself may pull an employee aside to point out a flaw and suggest a better way of doing something next time. Training, he says, requires more of a commitment of time than of money, meaning that organizations with a budget that's only a fraction of his restaurant's can still afford to make the investment. Training, he believes, is the best opportunity to inculcate a culture built around high standards of service in food and wine.

"The wine and beverage service training at Trotter's is first-rate. There's a strong mentoring program where the wine service veterans spend time teaching, both formally and informally, the less-experienced members of the wine team and the general service team. I like the way his people teach each other."

—Fred Dame, Master Sommelier

SPARING NO EXPENSE

A half dozen bottles of dessert and late harvest wines—each of which would command a price of $100 or more in the restaurant—were about to be sacrificed.

Bottles of Sauternes, sherry, and amontillado—wines that put a sweet finishing touch on an evening at Trotter's—awaited twenty front-of-the-house staffers attired in crisp white chef's jackets, seated at a large table in the studio kitchen. But this was to be no bacchanal. Wine training at Trotter's is serious business.

All had come to the weekly ninety-minute training session armed with notebooks; some also toted *Sotheby's Wine Encyclopedia* or *The Oxford Companion to Wine*. Dog-eared notes were stuffed into several of their encyclopedias. The service team members, as they always are at the Thursday afternoon wine training sessions, were joined by a handful of representatives from the kitchen. The wine service training sessions begin more than three hours before evening service; so do the Tuesday food service training sessions.

For Trotter, the time and expense of training is a savvy investment. "I never ask myself: 'How much is this costing me?' A half dozen bottles of good wine is a very small price to be paid for the twenty to twenty-five people who attend the training. It's the price of getting an employee from point A to point B. You can't put a price on that. These employees, be they from the front of the house or the kitchen, now have new insights into a wine or a dish we may be serving."

Wine and food are not only studied by the staff but also tasted in order to gain a deeper understanding and appreciation of what they're putting in front of the guests. Because anyone on the staff is capable of doing just about anything at any time, the service team is meticulously cross-trained, which discourages territorialism and engenders versatility and a tag team–like spirit of teamwork.

JACKS OF ALL TRADES

A food runner, a receptionist, a server assistant, or a primary server— all must know the wine and the food. Any one of them may be asked by a guest about the wine or the food. Guests would have a hard time distinguishing a food runner from a sommelier because every member of the dining room team wears a dark blue, black, or gray business suit. In the early years of the restaurant, the waitstaff wore uniforms while the wine team members wore dark suits. "We decided to put everyone in business suits because they are service professionals. They are no different from the people who dress in suits and go downtown every day," Trotter notes.

It goes without saying that the sommeliers are food connoisseurs. Likewise, the kitchen staff must have well-tuned palates for wine and insight on the fine points of service in the dining room. At the very least, every employee in the restaurant requires expertise in service, in wine, and in food—and that's not an inexpensive proposition.

The staff is trained for both breadth and depth of knowledge in food and wine. But four members of the front-of-the-house staff are always designated as the wine service team—two senior sommeliers and two of more junior status. One of the key missions of the specialized unit is to meet the needs of the 20 percent of the guests who are highly knowledgeable and well experienced with wine. "I need a team of people who are equally knowledgeable about wine and who have the ability to talk with those guests about producers, regions, and vintages," Trotter explains.

"We have some super-sophisticated guests whose great passions in life are great food, great wine, great restaurants, great travel. They read the food and wine publications and they visit the famous wineries or the well-known restaurants. They know as much as or more than the average sommelier, and they enjoy challenging sommeliers on their wine knowledge. Some people follow the great sommeliers just like they follow the great chefs. I have seen that with Larry Stone. We have to be ready to meet their needs. But for the other 80 percent of our guests, our servers can do a fine job for them." The fact is that servers at Trotter's can usually run circles around the sommeliers at many fine dining restaurants.

Trotter estimates that 80 percent of the guests order wine. The other 20 percent will not because of allergies, because they may be recovering from an addiction, or because of some moral objection. Those guests will opt for the Beverage Tasting Menu or water, coffee, or tea.

A PORTFOLIO OF RESPONSIBILITIES

The wine service team members have other responsibilities, including procuring the wine and other beverages, maintaining the cellars and the stemware, providing staff training, and conducting wine tastings for the staff. They also play important roles in Trotter's Excellence Program, which introduces Chicago-area grammar and high school students to a fine dining experience.

"Trotter has engendered a sense of professionalism in the staff. And it's a staff that supports each other as a team. Trotter's preservice meetings are wonderful. It's not dictatorial in the least. It's the staff talking to each other, asking 'How can we do tonight's service better than we did last night's?' They have the ability to be self-critical."

— Evan Goldstein, Master Sommelier and author of *Perfect Pairings: A Master Sommelier's Practical Advice for Partnering Wine with Food*

The multicourse meal, sans wine, is free, just like the advice Trotter's sommeliers and other staffers give the students about the exuberance and passion they bring to their jobs. Groups of students visit the restaurant three times a week during the school year. The big yellow school buses parked in front of Trotter's on Armitage Avenue are a sure sign that the Excellence Program is in session.

The highlight of the visit, according to sommelier Molly Wismier, is the trip to the wine cellars; the students, like many of their adult counterparts, are eager to see the cellars' crown jewels, like the bottle of Château Lafite Rothschild 1870.

INDULGING IN A NATURAL CURIOSITY

Alex Bachman's first job in the restaurant was cleaning the floors of the wine cellars; after that he moved through the ranks to a junior position on the wine service team. Bachman says the training sessions remind him how little he knows about the world of wine. But the sessions have also whetted his appetite to learn more about the wine-growing regions, the producers, the varietals, the vintages, and the science of winemaking. Bachman, a history graduate of nearby DePaul University, said he finds wine and its history fascinating—undoubtedly a valuable curiosity for someone planning a career in the wine field.

Role-playing exercises, a centerpiece of the wine service training, have been enormously helpful when the curtain rises for an evening of service, Bachman says. "I've been caught off-guard a few times by a situation or a question from a guest. But with the experience and the training, I feel better prepared for challenges in the dining room."

The training is tough, especially the role-playing. In one session, Linda Violago, a former Trotter's sommelier who was pitching in at the restaurant during a busy period around the holidays, provided instruction on technical aspects of service. She called on a server to deliver stemware to a tableful of his colleagues who were playing the role of guests. He carefully balanced four stems on a silver tray and placed them at specific positions on the table.

Although the glassware seemed to go down flawlessly, Violago wasn't completely satisfied with the server's performance. She admonished him about reaching over the guest and invading his or her personal space. "Try to be less intrusive when you deliver something to the table," she said. Then she provided a quick demonstration, based on her twenty-plus years of dining-room experience, on how not to interrupt a table. Her audience was rapt.

A MINIMALIST APPROACH

Christian Giles, a Trotter's veteran and the dining room manager, explained that precision usually entails executing as few moves as possible on the floor. By eliminating unnecessary steps in the close quarters of the dining room, servers reduce the chance that they'll clang glasses, collide with each other, or brush up against a guest.

The server remained on the hot seat as sommelier Conrad Reddick, who majored in mechanical engineering at the University of Illinois and who usually takes the lead instructional role at the sessions, invited him to demonstrate how he would open a bottle of wine. With his wine key, the server properly cut the capsule, inserted the corkscrew, and levered out the cork.

He earned a good grade as he delicately placed a cloth napkin on the underside of the bottle while displaying the label and stating the name of the wine to the table of his role-playing colleagues. Reddick advised him to set the cork straight up on a small dish to the guest's right, otherwise it would roll off the table. He also told his students that they should ask the guest for permission to remove the cork from the table, noting that some guests keep it as a souvenir. He added that the server or sommelier can offer the wine bottle's label to the guests. He returned to his seat, and the training session turned to the science of properly arranging the stemware, flatware, and silverware.

That session was technically focused; others, such as the dessert wine workshop, are designed to broaden a service team's wine knowledge and help refine their palates. One of the key goals of the training is to give the service staff the confidence to speak knowledgeably about wine at the table. Some guests, having established a comfortable rapport with their server, will want to talk about wine only with that person.

A few guests, who may be intimidated by the stereotype of the high-handed sommelier who will only underscore their ignorance of wine, do not want a visit from a sommelier. Trotter finds that unfortunate. In fact, sommeliers at Trotter's make it a point not to introduce themselves as the sommelier. They merely present themselves as someone who can provide them with additional guidance and assistance with the wine. "It would be arrogant of me to come to the table and tell the guests that I'm the sommelier," says Molly Wismier.

PUTTING THEIR TASTE TO THE TEST

All wine service team members, including Bachman, played instructional roles in the dessert wine session by leading the tasting of each wine and providing detailed wine notes on each selection. Staffers from both the front and the back of the house were called on to describe what they saw, smelled, and tasted from each sampling of the wine.

Another server described what she perceived to be notes of citrus, peach, pineapple, lychee nuts, and apricots, even a touch of acid. "That's the beauty of Sauternes," Violago responded with enthusiasm. "It's sweet with a kick of acid. It has a nice long finish. Some would say it has the taste of caramel." Reddick made the point that the dessert wines are as carefully matched to the desserts as wines are to the savory cuisine. He encouraged his students that day to make recommendations that are informed by their knowledge of the wine and food.

Other training sessions are designed to prepare the staff for a particular evening, such as the restaurant's New Year's Eve celebration, which was to be a departure from a regular night's service because food would be served not at the table but from stations scattered through the restaurant's dining areas and wine cellars.

It's critical to convey a sense of enthusiasm when conducting a training session, says Reddick; otherwise the staff reacts with indifference and less information is absorbed. Take the training session for the New Year's Eve party. Tables and credenzas were removed from the restaurant to make way for the temporary food stations and a dance floor. Reddick wanted the staff to be on its toes for what would be an exciting and unusual evening. In the past, New Year's Eve had been treated as any other night of dining, notwithstanding the extra Champagne being poured.

At the special session, he handed the service team a sheet with the wine selections that would be offered at the celebration. It began with a Moët & Chandon Brut Imperial and ended on a big note in the form of a fifteen-liter Veuve Clicquot Brut Yellow Label. Reddick, Wismier, and Violago walked the staff though the wines, commenting on their flavor profiles, vintages, and the backgrounds of their producers.

The battle plan for that evening called for Riedel Champagne glasses for the sparkling wine and Riedel Overture glasses for the still wine, because that style allows guests to assess the flavor profile of a number of different varietals. Although there would be only two types of stemware in play that evening, Reddick noted that they anticipated going through a lot of stemware, and the kitchen's stemware polishers needed to be at the ready.

WEARING ENTHUSIASM ON THEIR SLEEVES

Reddick encouraged the service team to be enthusiastic and spontaneous on New Year's Eve, despite the fact that the staff would be just as focused as it was on any normal night at the restaurant. That training session ended on a high note as Reddick muscled the large-format bottle of Veuve Clicquot onto the credenza in the middle of the dining room. Staffers surged forward to admire the enormous Nebuchadnezzar bottle. The drilling and the preparation for the special night paid off as the wine, the food, and the service all gelled.

Chef de cuisine Matthias Merges, who occasionally works the front of the house, attends many of the wine service training sessions because he considers them vitally important to the success of the restaurant. "Everyone here must have as broad a knowledge base as possible. That makes all of them more confident of their ability to achieve the kind of technical prowess that our guests expect."

A well-trained staff with the confidence to handle a variety of tasks, including describing and pouring the wine, is especially important on busy weekend evenings when the sommeliers are in great demand. "We don't want guests to have to wait for a sommelier to become available. We want this to be as seamless as possible, which is why we want any service person to be able to handle a wine order. You meet the demand with a well-trained staff."

In addition to the formal training sessions on Thursdays, Merges will arrange more impromptu sessions for the service team to sample ingredients and get a sense for what goes with what, either in the kitchen or at the bar in the restaurant's foyer. He's a strong advocate of staffers learning more about food and wine by exposing themselves to sources outside the restaurant. He encourages members of both sides of the house to take a wine class, visit other top restaurants, join a wine club, or drop in on tastings around Chicago or even when they are out of town on vacation.

ART FOR ART'S SAKE

"There's only so much you can learn here," Merges explains. "In fact, on their days off, we encourage our chefs to spend a few hours at the Art Institute, for example, just to open their minds to something new. Or when they are traveling, I like them to pay careful attention to what's around them. When they come back here, they have a greater appreciation for what we are trying to do. They come back here and see things differently, from a new and fresh perspective."

Trotter says he expects his sommeliers to be not only great wine stewards, but also great teachers. It's part of the legacy of Larry Stone and Joe Spellman. "Larry was constantly cajoling and prodding people here to be inquisitive about the wine and the food. He was always asking what they thought about a wine and what they liked or disliked about it. He pressed them to get a sense for whether they thought, for example, that a Sauvignon Blanc went with a certain cheese. Joe was the same way. They were provocateurs with their staffs, but they were never out to embarrass anyone. They were never elitist or pedantic." Stone and Spellman would often arrange blind tastings for the staff to enhance their wine knowledge.

They were the only ones who were hired specifically to be sommeliers. Since then, wine service team members, including sommeliers, have had to work their way through the ranks. And even Stone and Spellman paid their dues by running food and waiting tables along with their responsibilities as sommeliers. Boot camp for future wine service team members typically begins by running food to the tables—a humble beginning for someone who a couple of years later may be opening $10,000 bottles of wine or procuring wines from some of the great châteaux of Europe!

Wismier had been a sommelier at a respected fine dining restaurant in Chicago. But she wanted to take her career to another level and applied at Trotter's. She was hired and soon found herself running food, which she says was an invaluable experience because it familiarized her not only with the food and how it's paired with the wine but also with the various tables and dining rooms in the restaurant. The experience also gave her a sense for the rhythm of the restaurant.

LEARNING HOW TO RUN

A candidate who expresses an interest in wine service at Trotter's and who's hired will begin as a food runner. But he or she will learn much more than just how to carry plates from the kitchen into the dining rooms. At the twice-weekly food and wine training sessions, the service team member will begin to develop expertise. Trotter and his team leaders are quick to recognize an employee who seems to have a flair for and a fascination with wine and serving it to the guests.

"I would look for such things as how well they're doing in training and tasting sessions," says Trotter. "Are they genuinely interested? Are they psyched to learn new skills? I would look for their service aptitude at or around tables. I would watch to see how rapidly their technical skills are developing. But what I really look for is a sense of sheer enthusiasm, and it's little things that give off the right signals. It could be as simple as the flourish with which a staff person pours a wine in a training session rather than someone simply going through the motions. I certainly don't want someone who sees the job as sommelier as an opportunity to be a wine snob. I want someone who is humble and who genuinely cares about the guest."

On a few occasions, a front-of-the-house employee who may not have expressed an interest in becoming a member of the wine service team gets a tap on the shoulder from Trotter or one of his leaders who recognize great potential in a staffer. "I might tell the staff person that I noticed how much they appear to be enjoying interacting with the guests or how inquisitive they have been at training sessions."

Trotter says one of the most critical tasks of a restaurateur or any leader is recognizing the potential and the passion of a staff member amid the bustle and distractions of normal operations. Organizations rise and fall on their ability to identify and nurture talent and develop a next generation of leadership.

GOING BEYOND THE CALL

Dining room manager Christian Giles says another strong indicator of candidacy for the wine service team is a staff person's willingness to go the extra mile—by, for example, volunteering to work at a special luncheon at the restaurant, at a private event in a person's home where the Trotter's dining experience is recreated, or at a book signing at Trotter's To Go, where an extra hand on the wine side is always appreciated. Book signings or other special events can serve as introductions to celebrity chefs or famous sommeliers. Once a person becomes a member of the wine service team, the staffer is expected to attend wine tastings or other wine events on his or her own time. In most cases, he says, the person needs no encouragement; it's exactly what she or he would most want to do that day.

Leaders at Trotter's say they look for new or special assignments that are within or slightly beyond the capability of the staff member. It can be done at any restaurant or in any setting, they say. The key is giving the staff person the resources to succeed.

They watch carefully for a spark of interest on a staff member's part. For example, a new server may be observed speaking to guests with great enthusiasm about California chardonnays. The server would be offered the opportunity to attend an upcoming wine tasting in Chicago featuring California chardonnays as a way of preparing the server to take a leading role in organizing a wine event at the restaurant. It's a form of motivation, of pushing that staff member to the next level—perhaps becoming a member of the wine team. Trotter's loves to challenge its staff and discourage complacency by putting opportunities before them.

Giles, who participates in the hiring process with Trotter and Merges, agrees that it can be a bad sign when a candidate for a front-of-the-house position says he wants to start as a sommelier. Quite a few applicants have wine service experience in their backgrounds; some, like Wismier or Serafin Alvarado, had already been sommeliers when they came on board. New hires from restaurants with well-regarded wine programs are often amazed at how much more the servers or even the server assistants know about wine than they do. It's not unusual for servers at Trotter's to pull corks on $1,000 bottles during the course of an evening.

"But the answer is 'no' if the candidate wants to come straight in as a sommelier," Giles says. "There's simply too much to learn, and we want people who are willing to make the investment in learning how it's done here. We want people who want to work as a team rather than for themselves. We tell them it will be at least a year, maybe two years before someone can advance to sommelier here. The food and wine pairing is so important here. The wine service people have to understand how a dish is sauced. Most important, our sommeliers are the eyes and ears of the restaurant. They have to understand everything that goes on in both the kitchen and the dining rooms. The job is not for everyone."

Giles says a sommelier must be not only sensitive to every nuance in the restaurant during service, but also able to withstand the physical rigors of operating on three floors of the restaurant—from the wine cellars to the kitchen and dining rooms on the first floor to the two dining rooms on the second floor. The pace is fast, although never harried—at least as perceived by the guests. Before and after service, sommeliers are moving cases of wine, stemware, and anything else that must find its proper place.

THANKS, BUT NO THANKS

When told of the apprenticeship that awaits them, some candidates intent on becoming a sommelier say they're no longer interested. They've spared themselves and the restaurant the mutual disappointment. Giles says some candidates who express an initial preference for wine service find they're happy with primary service, which has its share of wine service responsibilities. Servers have ample opportunities to describe and pour wine.

As noted, a new hire's first assignment will be on the run team, which consists of three to five staffers who whisk the plates from the kitchen and then, with an understated flair, simultaneously place them before all the guests at a table. In the kitchen, as they await the plates, they are expected to pay close attention to how the chefs are plating the food. They must hover close enough to the expediting station so they can overhear the conversations between the sommeliers and the expediting chef about wine and food pairings and all the adjustments taking place throughout the evening. Runners also should observe how service takes place at the restaurant's kitchen table, where two sets of guests each evening are feted with a twelve-course degustation menu.

In the dining room, their antennae must be well tuned. They need to be aware, for example, of a guest who has left the table to visit the washroom. That will affect the pace at the table, which has a spillover effect in the kitchen—if the kitchen is aware that a guest has left the table. The sommelier or the primary server will undoubtedly be aware of the guest's status and alert the kitchen, but nothing can be left to chance.

THE NEXT RUNG UP THE LADDER

After several months of running food, the staffer typically advances to work at the front door, where she or he greets the guests in the foyer and escorts them to their table. "We're looking for a certain tableside manner from the person who's now interacting more closely with the guests. We want to see how rapidly their skills develop at that level," says Giles, who points out that a sense of courtesy and empathy should be second nature to the staffer. If not, then it becomes obvious that Trotter's made the wrong hire. But in most cases, it's been the right hire.

Another path toward advancement is as a server assistant, a role that supports the primary servers in the dining room. There is one server assistant per room who helps set and clear tables and is ready to pitch in on any aspect of the service. Staffers who seem averse to teamwork at that level will see their progress slow or stop altogether. The assignment, which lasts several months, gives the server assistant an intimate appreciation of how everything unfolds during the course of the evening. The server assistant begins to grasp the importance of not just reacting to a guest's needs, but also anticipating what the guest may want. It's a well-honed skill among Trotter's primary server and sommelier corps.

NAVIGATING THE GUEST'S EXPERIENCE

The next step in the staffer's progress is the role of primary server, responsible for everything that goes on at a table during the course of the three-hour dining experience. A primary server is conversant with the food and the wine and has developed an intuitive sense for what the guest wants or may want. He or she is expected to be

---

PREPARING FOR THE COURT

Members of the wine service team at Trotter's are a studious lot. They're often studying for a course or an exam offered by the Court of Master Sommeliers, the leading international examining body.

Established in England in 1977 to encourage high standards for beverage knowledge and service, the Court of Master Sommeliers has three levels of certification: Introductory, Advanced, and Master. Sommeliers at Trotter's have completed their advanced coursework. Some of the servers have completed introductory level coursework.

The Court administers the Master Sommelier diploma exam only to those who have passed a stringent series of courses and exams. The exam is offered by invitation only, and only about 10 percent of those who qualify to take the exam pass it. There are only 130 Master Sommeliers in the world, about 80 in the United States.

Five of them have worked at Trotter's. Larry Stone arrived with his MS in hand; Joe Spellman and Serafin Alvarado earned theirs while working at Trotter's. Brian Cronin and Jason Smith began their MS studies at Trotter's, but earned their diplomas while at other restaurants.

Several other sommeliers at Trotter's have earned the Advanced diploma. They have all done it on their own time, although they are given time off to sit for exams. Trotter pays for the courses and exam fees.

His wine service staff's success in the Court of Master Sommeliers is a source of enormous pride for Trotter. "We have employed, graduated, or helped graduate more Master Sommeliers in the United States than any other restaurant by far."

He is especially proud of the fact that his people excel at the service portion of the intensive three-part MS exam, which also includes a written test on wine knowledge and a blind tasting of six wines.

For an organization to grow and to prosper, it's essential that its employees join professional associations and attend training programs or earn professional designations. Trotter encourages members of his wine team to take the CMS courses and seek the professional designations. He and members of his staff are active in the organization's activities.

---

poised and well-spoken and must bring a finely honed set of technical skills to the table.

The primary server must be able to marshal any resource in the restaurant at a moment's notice to create a transcendent experience for the guest. Trotter says the job can best be described as that of a navigator. It's a tall order, and it doesn't include the additional responsibilities of being a junior member of the wine service team.

A less formal form of education and training takes place every night during service. Any service person in a dining room is expected to remain focused on the task at hand and also to lend an ear to what's being said by the sommelier. Reddick says conversations he's having with guests about wine are valuable for the service staff. A staff person can get a stronger sense for the kind of information being exchanged between the sommelier and the guest from that conversation. It's not a role-playing exercise at that point.

A newer member of the wine team will assist with the binning, inventory, and other responsibilities in the cellars. They arrive early and stay late. They play instructional roles at wine training sessions, and they are expected to develop a command of wine by reading industry journals, wine encyclopedias, and news accounts, and by visiting Web sites devoted to wine.

At a preservice meeting one evening, Alex Bachman brought along a rich-looking, four-color brochure that a wine producer had sent to the restaurant. He showed it to Reddick, who like a teasing older brother told Bachman he could add the brochure to his personal collection, but only if he could identify the types of rocks and soil depicted on the cover. Bachman's answers didn't seem to satisfy Reddick. He good-naturedly snatched the brochure from Bachman, who learned a valuable lesson in *terroir*. As Trotter says, the training and education at his restaurant are perpetual.

Reddick and other leaders at the restaurant are known to impart or reinforce lessons at any point during service and during preservice meetings. At one meeting, he admonished the service staff for their apparent lack of familiarity with the wines on the accompaniment menu the night before. He said he had overheard some of the servers providing superficial descriptions of the wines in response to guests' questions. To make his point, he brandished that evening's list of wines on the accompaniment and randomly called on members of the service team to describe certain selections. It was a mixed performance, with a couple of red-faced staffers apologizing for their ignorance and vowing to do better.

SERVICE POINTS

Charlie Trotter makes sure a sommelier has the right stuff when he hires one. Soft skills are innate, he believes. Training helps build on those natural talents. When hiring and training, an owner or manager should consider these service points:

- Hire people with soft skills such as empathy, a sense of hospitality, enthusiasm, genuineness, curiosity, graciousness, and intuition, which are impossible to teach.

- Look for candidates who have the potential to play a variety of roles at any time in the restaurant.

- Cross-train to discourage territorialism and create a tag team–like spirit of teamwork.

- To be certain the candidate is genuinely interested in the position, paint the darkest possible picture of a service role at the restaurant.

- Give candidates the opportunity to observe service or shadow a wine service team member for several nights as they consider taking a position at the restaurant.

- Make sure training is perpetual and takes many forms: lectures, role-playing exercises, wine tastings, and trips to the field. Trotter's holds weekly food service training every Tuesday and wine service training every Thursday.

- Candidly and constructively critique a staffer's performance in a variety of situations through role-playing of scenarios they are likely to encounter on the floor. This lessens the chance the staffer will be caught off guard.

- In training sessions, always convey a sense of enthusiasm for the topic or product; otherwise, the staff may react indifferently and absorb less information.

- Encourage service team members who want to specialize in wine service to volunteer for special events to enhance their knowledge and demonstrate to management their genuine interest.

- Instruct staffers to consciously listen in on conversations the sommeliers are conducting with the guests; in this way they can gain valuable service lessons.

4

On-the-Road Training

Harvesting Insights from Vineyards and
Tasting Rooms

To overcome the limited educational value of the sales calls that winemakers and distributors make at the restaurant, Trotter sends members of his wine and culinary teams into the field to experience firsthand how a foodstuff or a wine is made.

It's not an inexpensive proposition, Trotter acknowledges, but it's an investment in his staff that pays off many times over. In the course of a week in March 2007, for example, Trotter's lead sommeliers, Conrad Reddick and Molly Wismier, visited nearly twenty wineries in the Napa and Sonoma valleys of Northern California. In their absence, senior dining room managers and the junior members of the wine service team piloted wine service in Chicago.

Reddick and Wismier weren't dispatched to the nation's premier wine-growing region simply to gain an appreciation for the lay of the land, however. They were also there to learn the stories about how the grapes were grown and vinified, the history, the romance, the inside stories that, when shared with guests, add so much to making the food and wine experience at Trotter's memorable.

Wismier says the opportunity to walk the soil of the vineyards, to meet the winemakers, and to taste their handiwork is invaluable, not only for her professional education as a sommelier but for the guest as well. Armed with that knowledge and experience, Wismier can better share the romance of a wine, a varietal, a vintage, or even an entire region in the time she spends with a guest at tableside. Even if she's with them for no more than a minute, she says her insights can substantially enhance the guest's experience, especially if the guest is fascinated with wine. She can speak more authoritatively and passionately about the wine, having met the winemaker, the vineyard manager, or the winery owner. Each has a story to tell.

The winery visits are also an opportunity for the sommeliers to further calibrate their already-sophisticated palates. "It's important that we train our senses," she says. The sharper the sommeliers' antennae, the less likely it is that a guest will be presented with a bottle that is anything less than it should be. The sommeliers, who taste each bottle in the dining room before it's served to a guest, will quickly recognize if a wine is not living up to its standards and make the appropriate adjustment.

INTO THE HILLS

On the first day of their weeklong visit, Reddick and Wismier turned their car off the famous Silverado Highway and drove up a series of switchbacks into the foothills overlooking the Napa Valley. Their ears popped as the ascent continued through a lunar landscape of rubble and stony outcroppings of brown and burnt orange.

The destination was a forty-five-acre mountainside parcel planted with cabernet sauvignon grapes by Joseph Phelps Vineyards. The iron-rich, steeply terraced plot's location spoke volumes about the character of the wine from Phelps' grand cru, estate-owned Backus Vineyard.

In the gathering dusk of a late winter's afternoon several weeks before bud break, Reddick and Wismier harvested insights about the vineyard and the struggle the vines faced in that seemingly harsh environment. Guiding them through the vineyard was Damian Parker, Phelps' vice president of production, and Ashley Hepworth, associate winemaker and former member of Trotter's culinary staff in Chicago.

Reddick is particularly fond of wine produced from mountainside vineyards because at higher altitudes grapes bask in an intense sun, but they don't bake from the high temperatures they could experience at a lower elevation. Acid content tends to be greater at higher elevations, and the drainage patterns on a mountainside minimize the risk of the grapes becoming oversaturated with water. The rocky terrain often requires the vines' root systems to struggle for nourishment, and that can produce a splendidly complex grape. Reddick notes that a vineyard down the hill might produce a completely different style of wine.

A TASTE OF THE SOIL

This vineyard's *terroir*—the sum of the various influences such as climate, angle of the sun, soil content, wind, and moisture—lends itself to a wine with concentrated flavors, a hint of minerality, and a boost in the wine's acidity. It's the kind of wine that is especially compatible with the food served at Charlie Trotter's. From his first impression of the parcel, Reddick discerned the characteristics of the wine produced from the Backus Vineyard near the Napa Valley community of Oakville.

The vineyard visit imparted insights that would be impossible to glean from a book or a Web site. Winemakers or their distributors, many hoping to find a coveted place on Trotter's wine list, eagerly visit Chicago to describe their wares to the sommeliers.

"A winemaker can visit us in Chicago, where we can pick up on his passion, but we are not at the winery," Reddick says. "When you are on the property you have a sense of place, the smell, the look. You can pick up on all the subtleties, such as the vineyard's cover crop like lilac or clover, which helps you understand why you may have been tasting those subtle notes in the wine."

Two to three distributors typically visit on Mondays when the restaurant is closed to guests. Many more distributors than the restaurant can accommodate request a meeting. During the sales calls, the sommeliers taste the wines that are being offered. In addition to tastings, Reddick says he will discuss with the distributor the winemaker's philosophy, viticultural practices, and pricing. He will often ask what makes the wine special and how long it's been in the bottle.

It's important to have a strong professional relationship with distributors, Reddick says. "I'm interested in what the distributor can do for the restaurant. I want to be certain that the wine is delivered to the restaurant in the proper condition, I want the most competitive pricing possible, and I want them to be willing to supply wine for special events at no cost or at a reduced price."

Smaller restaurants, Reddick says, should make themselves available to as many distributor calls as possible because many distributor reps are highly knowledgeable about the industry and important trends. Some of them are former sommeliers or beverage managers.

ROMANCING THE GRAPE

Distributor calls are convenient, but again, they don't offer the insights of a site visit. "The best part of those kinds of trips is that you get to know the people behind the wines that you are serving," Reddick says. "You understand how much effort goes into producing the wine. You get a sense for the passion and the tradition at each winery."

As he does with his culinary team, Trotter occasionally sends his wine team into the field to gain firsthand knowledge of the products they are selling. It's an expense not many restaurants can afford, but if the budget permits, it's always money well spent because of the valuable insights and contacts produced by the trips.

The educational process began earlier that day in the tasting room at the Phelps winery in St. Helena. Parker described the blend and grape sources for many of its wines, including its 2005 Sauvignon Blanc, 90 percent Sauvignon and 10 percent Semillon. Grapes were harvested at 23 degrees Brix (a measure of the percentage of sugar in the grape) and aged for nine months in two- to three-year-old French oak barrels.

Wismier, who scribbled dutifully into a notebook, said that it is important for a sommelier to be aware of those kinds of influences on a wine in order to better train her senses. While she jotted, Reddick and Parker discussed Phelps' biodynamic agricultural program on about ninety acres of its vineyards in Napa Valley to ecologically enhance the natural vineyard environment through such practices as introducing a variety of farm animals, such as sheep or chickens, into the vineyards. They help contribute to the harmonious interaction of vegetation, soil, insects, and each other, Parker explained.

> "You have to keep up, and you have to keep learning, and Trotter's people have managed to do that."
>
> —Fred Dame, Master Sommelier

He also discussed drainage practices, fermentation practices, and the *cépages* or blends of varietals that go into each of the Phelps' wines. The sommeliers tasted a series of Phelps' wines during a discussion of the Phelps' winemaking philosophy. "We are all farmers," Parker said of his fellow winemakers. "We are all looking for practices that have made other farmers successful."

The day ended with an evening at The French Laundry, the renowned Napa Valley restaurant of Chef Thomas Keller. The meal, an extravagant sixteen-course tasting menu brilliantly paired with a progression or *flight* of wines, was both a reward and an opportunity for the sommeliers to experience superlative service from a different perspective. Trotter encourages his staff to visit some of the better restaurants or hotels when they are on the road so they can bring fresh ideas back to Trotter's. The meal had a profound impact on Reddick and Wismier, who were inspired by the precision and graciousness of The French Laundry's food and wine service.

LESSONS AT THE FEET OF THE MASTER

The longest visit during the trip was with Master Sommelier Larry Stone, now general manager of the Rubicon Estate in Napa Valley. Reddick and Wismier spent nearly a full day with Stone and came away with a semester's worth of wine knowledge. Stone was eager to help educate the sommeliers who inherited his legacy at Trotter's.

It would have been easy for Reddick and Wismier to feel intimidated in Stone's presence as he described everything from the influence of heat in the viticulture process to the history of winemaking in the Napa Valley. His history lesson that day began at Rubicon.

He escorted Trotter's sommeliers through the 1,700-acre estate now owned by Academy Award–winning film director Francis Ford Coppola. The estate's winemaking history dates back to the nineteenth century when it produced the famous Inglenook wines. The estate was purchased in 1879 by Gustave Niebaum, a Finnish ship captain who made a fortune in Alaskan furs.

Stone explained that Niebaum wasn't interested in making a profit from the winery, but only to make an outstanding wine. In the late nineteenth century, California wines were considered inferior to the more established European vintages. Niebaum set out to change that by producing award-winning wines under the Inglenook label. His winery came to produce wine that could rival some of the best from France's Bordeaux and Burgundy regions. The

GETTING THE INSIDE STORY

Learning a winemaker's philosophy firsthand, tasting the wine, or walking the vineyards is an invaluable experience for a sommelier, who can then better appreciate the aesthetics of the locale and the technical nuances of what's in the bottle.

For some reason, says Conrad Reddick, wine tastes different there, its characteristics more vibrant and more evident in the winery than it does in the restaurant. Winery visits allow the sommelier to better calibrate his or her senses to the wine's true nature and know exactly what it should taste like when it's being poured for a guest in the restaurant. A fault in the wine becomes easier to recognize.

Elements that Trotter's sommeliers are especially aware of on a winery visit include:

- *Microclimates:* Is the vineyard influenced by cool ocean breezes or warm valley air?

- *Soil conditions:* Is it rocky, sandy, or volcanic? Does water drain quickly or does it collect in the vineyard?

- *Cooperage:* Is the wine aged in French oak or American oak? How large are the barrels? How old are the barrels? How long is the wine aged in the barrel?

- *Corks:* What quality control measures does the winery take to ensure that its corks are not contaminated by TCA?

- *Viticulture practices:* Is the vineyard treated with herbicides and pesticides or is it treated biodynamically?

- *History:* How old is the winery? Who founded it? Is the founder or the founder's family still involved? What's unique about the winery and its handiwork?

prize-winning Inglenook became the first estate-bottled wine in California. After Niebaum's death in 1908, his wife and later a grand-nephew continued to operate the winery until it was sold in 1964.

THE GODFATHER OF WINE

In 1975, Coppola, on the heels of his success with *The Godfather*, bought the Niebaum home and a small vineyard, intending to make wine as a hobby. That is, until the day in 1980 that winemaker Robert Mondavi and Coppola shared a bottle of 1890 Inglenook drawn from the basement of the home. This, Stone told the Trotter's sommeliers, made Coppola realize what a powerful winemaking legacy he had inherited.

Over the course of the next twenty years, Coppola acquired the vineyards of the original estate and restored the Inglenook winery, which now also houses a small museum of his film-related projects, including the Tucker automobile used in the eponymous film that he directed. The Niebaum-Coppola Estate was renamed Rubicon.

Stone led Reddick and Wismier to a ridge overlooking the Rubicon Estate, where he described the *terroir* that lends specific characteristics to the wine. He pointed to Mount St. John, a thousand-foot peak that overlooks the estate. Over the ages, rock and dirt have eroded from the mountain and spilled into the valley floor below. The soil has a strong element of slate, a mineral conducive to the growth of the cabernet sauvignon grape.

From the ridge, he pointed to the estate's Gio and Garden vineyards and described the wind patterns and the amount of sun and shade each vineyard experienced during the growing season. Stone drove the sommeliers along the dirt and gravel mountainside paths, past Coppola's Zoetrope Studio.

Reddick appreciated the estate tour and history lessons from Stone. "History is so important because it helps you understand a sense of place and all the romance that surrounds it. Larry conveyed to us the passion and the love that went into the care of the vines on this estate. It was important for us to learn more about Gustave Niebaum because he played such a pioneering role in the development of wine from California."

HISTORY IN A BOTTLE

The all-day seminar continued over lunch at Redd, a restaurant in the Napa Valley community of Yountville. Stone brought along two of the estate's wines, and he described the characteristics of each of the expensive cabernets over the meal.

Reddick recalls, "The time we got to spend with Larry was some of the most valuable on the trip because he is so knowledgeable about viticulture, winemaking, the vineyards, and the history of the region. I picked something up from everything he said."

More insights into the art and science of winemaking were to be had in the nearly twenty wineries the Trotter's sommeliers visited, including Opus One, the joint venture formed in 1980 between Baron Philippe de Rothschild of Château Mouton Rothschild in Pauillac, France, and Napa Valley vintner Robert Mondavi, which produces an ultra-premium wine of the same name with a daunting price tag. (Wine conglomerate Constellation Brands acquired the Robert Mondavi Corporation in 2004 and assumed 50 percent ownership of Opus One.) The winery itself is a stunning piece of architecture designed to embody elements from both California and France.

At this winery, which produces only about thirty thousand cases a year, staff aims to achieve perfection in its production standards. There are no mechanical pumps that would jostle the grapes; instead, the wine is moved by way of a gentle gravitational flow. In the tradition of first-growth wines from the Bordeaux region, the expensive barrels of French oak are never reused. On the day of the sommeliers' visit, Opus One's winemaker Michael Silacci explained that he and members of his team were meeting with fifteen coopers to conduct tastings to get a sense for the influence of their barrels on Opus One. Silacci said the relationship between the wood and the wine is a critical element in the wine's flavor.

"You have to keep up, and you have to keep learning, and Trotter's people have managed to do that."

—Fred Dame, Master Sommelier

To underscore the importance of precision and exacting standards, Silacci related how he had recently taken the Opus One cellar team to The French Laundry for a special luncheon. It was an opportunity for his team to gain an appreciation for the teamwork and commitment to excellence that have long distinguished The French Laundry's kitchen and front-of-house staff. Like Trotter, Silacci likes to expose his staff to organizations with an intense commitment to quality.

GOING GREEN IN THE VINEYARD

Another stop was the Robert Sinskey Vineyards, a more decidedly California winery reflecting the laid-back, thoughtful personality of its owner of the same name. Over lunch prepared by his wife, professional chef Maria Helm Sinskey, Rob Sinskey discussed the merits of biodynamic viticulture, a practice his winery began to embrace in the early 1990s. By eschewing the conventional practices that relied on chemicals, Sinskey said the more organic approach has produced more consistent yields and grapes with better color and flavor. The proof was in the pudding as he poured the sommeliers a series of wines from his vineyards.

The lunchtime conversation featured a variety of insights—from the lack of respect that the finicky Pinot Noir grape tends to command to the futility of a winemaker's attempting to "chase the market" by sculpting its product to meet the tastes of the leading critics. Sinskey's winemaking philosophy was simple: "Define your style and stick with it."

At Diamond Creek Vineyards—which produced the first California wine ever to sell for more than $100 a bottle—Boots Brounstein, widow of the winery's founder, Al Brounstein, proudly showed off the postcard-pretty eighty-acre estate, which features three contiguous vineyards, each with its own soil content. One vineyard is gravelly, the second volcanic, and the third consists of red rock. The grapes from each vineyard evidence their own unique characteristics.

But the more critical insight was the pride and the passion of Boots Brounstein for the land that she and her husband purchased in 1972. At the wheel of her four-wheel-drive vehicle, she drove the sommeliers past Diamond Creek and a small lake, then up the side of a terraced vineyard while recounting a series of wonderful stories about her family and friends who had so enjoyed the vineyards over the course of thirty-five years.

Brounstein brought the Diamond Creek to life for her guests, who'll now be able to share a small measure of the romance of that winery and others in the Napa Valley with their own guests at Charlie Trotter's. Like professors converting their fieldwork into classroom lectures, Reddick and Wismier, upon their return to Chicago, shared their experiences from America's premier wine-growing region and their conversations with the winemakers and vineyard managers with the staff through a series of presentations at the Thursday wine service training sessions.

SERVICE POINTS

The learning curve for a sommelier at a fine dining restaurant is steep. The learning process can be enhanced by experiencing first-hand some of the products for which the sommelier is responsible. Owners and managers should consider these service points:

■ Engender deeper insights into the world of wine by sending sommeliers into the field. It makes them more discriminating buyers of wine and enhances their knowledge and effectiveness at tableside. It's difficult to glean the same level of insight from a wine distributor's sales call to the restaurant or from reading a book or visiting a Web site.

■ Take staffers to restaurants or other institutions noted for their outstanding service. This allows your own staffers to compare notes and take away winning ideas.

5

Perfecting the Finer Points of Wine Service

Wine service at Trotter's is technically precise, yet as elegant as the wine itself.

It all begins with the presentation of the wine list by a server or sommelier. The guests, who have been presented the evening's food menu, are asked if they would like to see the wine list. Not every guest wants to.

Traditionally, if it was a couple dining in the restaurant, the list was presented to the man. But that's no longer presumed. Sommelier Conrad Reddick tends to play that choice by ear as he quickly gauges which of the two seems more enthusiastic when both are asked if they would like to see the list.

In a business-related meal, the person who has made the reservation is usually the person handed the list. The businessperson may have spoken to the sommelier over the telephone about wines for the evening in advance of the visit. Trotter's uses a table and guest management software system that tracks customer information. There are terminals at the host stand in each dining room. The reservationists can indicate in the notes section the name of the person who made the reservation. That's usually the person who will select wines that evening, but not always.

The receptionist will often verify on arrival which member of a business party will be responsible for the wine order and indicate that person to the sommelier.

If the sommelier isn't sure by the time the party is being seated, he or she will step to the table with the list and watch to see which guest asks for the list. If there's any uncertainty, the sommelier will simply ask: "Is there a certain person who will be responsible for selecting the wines this evening?"

A READING ASSIGNMENT

The leather-bound sixty-page list with a distinctive "T" emblazoned on the cover is handed to the guest or placed on the table in front of the guest. Atop the wine list is placed a second and much less hefty folder that details the evening's Wine Accompaniment and the Premium Wine Experience. Guests, especially those new to the restaurant, may fear they have their work cut out for them.

Always positioning themselves to the right of the guest, as per tradition, servers and sommeliers promptly describe to the guest what lies in front of them. First, the Wine Accompaniment and the Premium Wine Experience options are explained. Next, the staff person points out the "wine by the glass" section in the back of the main list, and finally the guest is shown the list's table of contents in the front to help with navigation.

Some guests may bypass the list, having already studied it online. Previous guests of the restaurant may have already made up their minds. And in other cases, the guests say they prefer to leave all the decisions up to the sommelier.

Diners who opt for the $100 Wine Accompaniment, which features artisanal, small-production winemakers from upstart regions, or the $250 Premium Wine Experience, which offers world-class wines from established regions, will have completed their order, although the sommelier will play an active role in the table's progression of wines. If guests choose to drink by the bottle or by the glass, the sommelier will help them make selections.

THE ETIQUETTE OF PRESENTATION

Once a selection is made, the bottle is brought to the table and presented to the guest who ordered it. With the label side up to allow the guest to inspect it, and a crisp white napkin supporting the underside of the bottle, the sommelier points out the varietal, producer, and vintage for New World wines. For Old World wines, it's appellation, producer, and vintage. The sommelier continues to operate from the guest's right-hand side. Food is served from the left. It's traditional, and it also allows the guests to know what direction the sommelier will approach them from throughout service. It's one more way of allowing the guest to relax.

The presentation of the wine not only confirms for the guest that the correct bottle has been brought to the table but also involves the guest in the theater of it all. All wine is opened at a credenza in the center of each dining room. Positioning is important to keep the guests involved in the process.

A sommelier sets the bottle on a portion of the credenza closest to the guests, and the wine's label faces them at all times. The sommelier never turns his or her back on the guests, attempting to remain open and facing the guest to enhance a sense of engagement.

Using a waiter's knife, the server or sommelier cuts the bottle's capsule and removes it along with the bottle's wire

"From a mechanical standpoint, Trotter's wine service is among the best I've seen. It's something as simple as the way they carefully pour the wine and follow up with the same precision on the re-pour."

—Evan Goldstein, Master Sommelier and author of *Perfect Pairings: A Master Sommelier's Practical Advice for Partnering Wine with Food* cage. The corkscrew is inserted and the cork is levered out of the bottle. To ensure the quality of the wine, the server or sommelier pours a small measure into a glass, sniffs, gently swirls it, takes another quick sniff and tastes it. Sommeliers do not call attention to their tasting, but guests inevitably watch the ritual with great interest. And that's fine with the sommelier, as it adds panache to the service. Trotter says the ritual needs to be subtle, never flamboyant.

If certain that the wine is not corked and its nose and taste are true, the sommelier approaches the table and pours a small amount into the host's glass. If, after tasting the wine, the guest nods or states approval, the sommelier will pour for the other guests, moving in a clockwise direction.

A THEATRICAL FLAIR

Once the wine has been poured for everyone at the table, the sommelier returns it to the credenza, label facing the guest. The ritual is intended to add a touch of elegance to the evening.

In addition, the sommelier will place the cork straight up on a small dish or coaster (to prevent it from rolling off) and present it to the guest for inspection. Oenophiles will sometimes roll the cork through their fingers to determine if it's brittle, suggesting it has not been in proper contact with the wine. Some may sniff it. Service people are told never to remove the cork from the guest's table without permission because some guests want to keep it as a souvenir.

Servers and sommeliers are also instructed to be as unobtrusive as possible at the table and be careful not to reach into the guests' space. They know to minimize movement around the table and swap only small amounts of information with their service partners.

A lot of communication among service team members in the guests' presence is done silently, using their eyes to convey a look of concern or dismay. A slight nod of the head or a subtle hand gesture can silently speak volumes about what needs to be done or who needs to be where. It's a remarkably graceful ballet considering that teams are assigned each night only during the preservice meeting. Trotter doesn't want service team members getting too familiar with each other's patterns, concerned that it could lead to boredom and complacency. He wants them to keep their edge each night. A flexible, cross-trained service staff can more easily form efficient, impromptu teams to handle special events at the restaurant or off-site events where the normal rhythms of service don't necessarily apply. And when staff members call in sick or leave the restaurant, those on duty can more easily handle the disruption.

Trotter believes that a team of jacks-of-all-trades has intimate knowledge of every task in the front of the house. It's counter-productive, he believes, for staff people to become overspecialized. Cross-training staff is more complicated and time-consuming, but ultimately it pays off with more seamless service that's rarely delayed by the need for a specialist to appear at a table.

The stage is set for the guests each evening by the service staff, which carefully arranges the silverware, flatware, and stemware at each table. Trotter's has two seatings each night requiring the dining rooms to be reset.

Silverware, flatware, and stemware are placed in exactly the same positions for each setting at a table. The water glass is positioned at twelve o'clock, above the dinner plate, or what's often called the base plate. The wine glass is positioned to the right of the water glass. When a flight of wines is being presented, staff continues to set the newest glass of wine next to the water glass. Partially consumed glasses of wine are pushed to the periphery in a roughly clockwise direction. If empty, the glasses are usually removed from the table. If there's any doubt, the service person should ask the guest if it's okay to remove the glass.

"It's important to use an organized, regimented system for a wine progression," Reddick says. "That allows any service person to immediately recognize the state of the wine progression. The proper positioning of the glasses also makes it more enjoyable for the

"There is a certain calm to how the wine service team conduct themselves. It's easy to get overwhelmed in an environment like that. For example, I was poured a wine that I felt was corked. The service person did not catch it. I called him over and he handled it very professionally."

—Evan Goldstein, Master Sommelier and author of *Perfect Pairings: A Master Sommelier's Practical Advice for Partnering Wine with Food*

guest." Servers and sommeliers respectfully handle the glasses by their stems so as not to smudge the bowls or flutes into which the wine or Champagne will be poured.

The service sequence is consistent throughout the evening: stemware is placed, the wine is poured, and the food is served. Guests usually have several minutes to enjoy the wine on its own before its pairing partner—the dish—arrives. The combination of the two is what creates the transcendent experience. When clearing, servers remove plates first. It's all like clockwork, although no one table is the same as the next. That's the challenge of wine service.

THE TOOLS OF THE TRADE

A stubborn cork and a determined sommelier: they are the source of enormous curiosity among diners some evenings at Charlie Trotter's.

But with the right tools, the sommelier will always get his cork. Conrad Reddick doesn't mind the additional pressure of a dining room full of people looking on as he struggles with a cork. He's well armed for the task.

Attached to his belt or stuffed into his pants pockets are two to three wine keys, a fourteen-inch Maglite, a knife, and a couple of extractors. Resembling a switchblade, the wine key or waiter's friend features a coiled corkscrew, a lever, and a small knife.

The wine key will effortlessly raise most corks. But there are times when the center of an older cork is being raised by the lever and the screw's coils, but the outer edges of the cork are adhering to the neck of the bottle. Then it's time for a two-pronged extraction device known as the Ah-So. The prongs are inserted between the outer edge of the cork and the inside of the neck. With a slow, slight twist, voilà! (Or better put, Ah so!) The entire cork emerges.

Sometimes older corks will shrink with age. To deal with these, another handy device is a broken cork extractor, which can retrieve a cork or part of a cork that has been pushed into the bottle in an ill-fated attempt to pull it out. Three long wires tipped with tiny claws are inserted into the bottle. Once the claws are beneath the cork, the extractor is pulled up with the cork in its grasp.

Reddick says there are two telltale signs of trouble. One is when he slices the foil on the neck of a bottle and senses it's excessively dry or dusty. A second sign is when he plunges a corkscrew into the cork and it begins to disintegrate. He then knows he is in for a battle, but he realizes it is all a part of the wine service at Trotter's.

There's none of this drama, of course, with bottles topped with screwcaps instead of corks. Some Australian winemakers, as well as producers in other parts of the world concerned about contaminated corks, have begun bottling with screwcaps, a development that traditionalists only sniff at. Less than 5 percent of the bottles at Trotter's are sealed with metal screwcaps, also known as Stelvin closures. No bottle has ever been rejected by Trotter's because it was sealed with a screwcap, and there has never been a guest who's complained that the bottle he or she bought was sealed with a screwcap rather than a cork. "Our guests trust us," Reddick says. "My primary concern is the quality of the wine, not the closure. The jury is still out as to whether it's better to seal a bottle with the traditional cork or a screwcap." Wines at the lower end of the price spectrum that see little bottle aging are more apt to be sealed with a screwcap than older, more elite wines that are sealed with cork, he says.

THE SKILLS OF A SURGEON

A variety of service challenges arise during the course of the evening that demand strong technical skills. In a restaurant with a cellar chockful of older wine, sommeliers will pull corks on well-aged bottles. The corks may not have aged as well as the wine itself; in that case, they are at risk of disintegrating at the touch of a corkscrew.

Trotter says he's always been amazed at the surgical precision of his sommeliers when faced with what's known as a crumbly cork. "I remember watching sommelier Larry Stone spending a half hour on a 1987 Château d'Yquem where the cork was so powdery that I was afraid if someone sneezed the cork would have blown away. With beads of sweat on his forehead and a look of total concentration, Larry moved the extractor by fractions of an inch to get the bottle opened." With all eyes in the dining room trained on the scene at the credenza, Stone was able to pull the cork.

Fragments of cork are not harmful to the wine, but guests don't like cork in the wine, especially an older wine that is costing them hundreds or thousands of dollars.

Sommeliers are adept at using cheesecloth to filter into a decanter a wine that has fragments of cork. Wine with sediment, often an older red, is decanted. The decanting also takes place at the credenza as a sommelier gently pours the contents of the bottle into a decanter. If done properly, the sediment in the bottle will remain there.

LETTING IT BREATHE

An older wine in need of decanting will be delicately pulled from the rack in the cellar, placed in a cradle to help minimize movement, and brought to the dining room, where it is presented to the host of the table. Once the host has confirmed it's the correct bottle, the sommelier brings it to the credenza just as a normal bottle of wine would be treated.

In a ritual of a drama and elegance, the sommelier lights a candle to illuminate the bottle so that the thin layers of wine can be seen as it's poured slowly into a decanter. If properly done, the sediment in the bottle will not spill into the decanter. Guests often marvel at the sommelier's precision and concentration.

Once the bottle is emptied into the decanter, it is placed on the credenza, its label facing the guests. The sommelier samples the decanted wine. If it meets his or her standards, the sommelier approaches the table and pours the host a sample, and service proceeds from there.

"The wine service at Trotter's is absolutely impeccable. There have been many incredible sommeliers and servers at the restaurant who have lived up to the high standards Charlie set for his wine program. He doesn't give his wine team a blank check and simply say 'Do what's best.' He's constantly coaching them and challenging them. He's right there with them."

—Emeril Lagasse

SERVICE POINTS

Wine service at Charlie Trotter's is precise and elegant. It may look effortless, but there's a well-defined structure that underlies it. To emulate that high level of performance, consider these service points:

- Present the wine list to the member of the couple who seems most interested in it. Don't presume that the man will make the selections. If both people seem equally interested, give them each a list.

- For business-related meals, present the wine list to the person who made the reservation and who may have already discussed wine selections with the sommelier.

- Train the staff on how to properly present to guests supplements to the wine list such as the Wine Accompaniment or the Premium Wine Experience. In a typical scenario, the sommelier or server displays the wine list to the guest and then may lay it on the table. The sommelier or server will then note there is an additional leather-bound folder with the Wine Accompaniment and the Premium Wine Experience. He or she will typically lay the supplement atop the regular wine list.

- Conduct wine service from the right-hand side of the guest. Not only is this traditional, but it also allows the guest to relax by knowing the direction from which the sommelier will always approach.

■ Taste each bottle before it's presented to the guest. A small sampling allows the sommelier to ensure the wine's quality and lends an elegant touch to the service. Sommeliers don't call attention to the tasting, but most guests will take note.

■ Be mindful of a guest's personal space at the table and attempt to minimize activity in the guest's immediate vicinity. Frequent interruptions may irritate and distract the guest.

■ Treat a bottle of wine with great care regardless of whether guests are present.

6

Intuitive Service

Reading the Mind of the Guest

The technical side of service is child's play compared to the vastly more complex human skills a wine service team must deploy at tableside, says Charlie Trotter.

Intuition, humility, clairvoyance, empathy, graciousness, sincerity, and enthusiasm are qualities essential to the success of a wine service professional at Trotter's. As noted earlier in this book, they are traits Trotter looks for when he hires and promotes. Soft skills are difficult, perhaps impossible, to teach; technical skills are not, he believes.

"Our wine service is only as good as the people we send to the guests' table. If they don't have the aptitude to relate well to the guest, then our wine list, all the incredible wines in the cellar, and our reputation as a food and wine destination mean nothing."

PRECISE YET PERSONAL

Chef de cuisine Matthias Merges says the worst possible person you could put on a wine service team is someone who is highly knowledgeable, technically proficient, even flawless, but somehow off-putting to the guest. "If you don't have a warm, genuine, and honest relationship with a table, then it's hard to imagine that it will be a very pleasant experience for the guest."

The stereotypical French sommelier—an arrogant scold in a starchy tuxedo—would not play well at Trotter's. Nor would someone who was judgmental or who had a tin ear for the guests' needs. A restaurant can serve superb food and wine in an elegant atmosphere, but if the guests are tense and made to feel self-conscious, they probably won't return. Nor will they speak highly of their experience. The sommelier's role can be critical in creating a sense of comfort for the guest, because he or she is responsible for so many delicate matters that evening.

Some guests are insecure about their knowledge of wine. The insecurities are magnified in certain situations, such as when a guest is hosting a dinner for business clients or in a more romantic setting in which a guest may be trying to impress a suitor. Some are terrified of the possibility of mispronouncing the name of a French or Italian wine in front of their fellow diners. Some are uncertain about the etiquette of being presented a wine and its cork, the tasting and the pouring.

FINESSING TOUCHY SUBJECTS

And, of course, there's the price of wine, which at Trotter's can range from the modest to the astronomical. But all those sensitive issues and others can be gracefully defused by a sommelier with a deft human touch.

Sommelier Molly Wismier says there can be a lot of trepidation about wine. "If I sense that, I make it immediately clear to the guests that it is my responsibility to guide them through the list. Based on certain descriptions of previous experiences, I can help them find a wine within the profile they have enjoyed in the past. Or I may get a sense for something new they might like. I try to read them as best that I can. I always reassure them that what's most important is that they order a wine they enjoy."

Wismier aims to be keenly perceptive of how much information her guests want from her. "I don't want to dominate their time here, because the three-hour dining experience is so much more than just the wine they are drinking." Imparting a wealth of wine information at the table takes time, which is a precious commodity on a night when there are 190 diners in the restaurant.

SENSING THE RIGHT SIGNALS

Former Trotter's sommelier Lisa Ehrlich-Giglio found that it was often best to let the guest drive the wine and food experience, but to still keep an ear to the ground for signals as to the direction they wanted to take. "If it was a romantic evening and I sensed the couple wanted to be alone as much as possible, I would minimize my presence at the table. Other guests may want you to take them through the entire service. You need the intuitive skills of a psychologist to make the right judgments about a table. Some guests may want you to describe the vinification of the wine you brought them, while others want to know a story about the winery's founder or they may want to know why the restaurant selected a particular wine for its list."

Serafin Alvarado, another former Trotter's sommelier, says he relied heavily on his dialogue with guests. He found lecturing to be counterproductive because a monologue provides the sommelier with too little information. "You have to be able to find the guest's comfort zone, but it's not that easy. The situation is unique at every table. You have to ask the right

"The sommeliers and the entire dining room team have a knack for anticipating the guests' needs before they even realize they want something. That's the true mark of hospitality, and it's what we are all striving for."

—Thomas Keller, chef-owner of The French Laundry and Per Se

questions. It's up to the sommelier to listen to all the nuances and subtleties in terms of what they like and don't like. The more the guest can tell me about their experiences and tastes, the more accurately I can recommend the appropriate wine."

If Alvarado suspected a table was not enjoying the dining experience, he would marshal the full resources of the restaurant to turn things around at the table. "You certainly can't go to the table and say: 'What's wrong?' That would only make things worse. I would subtly ask about the wine or ask if they are enjoying the fish course, and I learn that the guest doesn't really care for shellfish. And the next course also happens to be fish. I would go to the kitchen and ask them to switch the next course to quail. Or I might pour them a wine that is completely out of the blue. It could be a flight of Pinot Noirs from three different regions just to demonstrate that we care about them as guests."

> "The magic to Trotter's wine service goes beyond the mechanics. The wine service team has the psychological and social skills to read and engage the guest. Ultimately, that allows the guests to make the possible wine selections for themselves."
>
> — Evan Goldstein, Master Sommelier and author of *Perfect Pairings: A Master Sommelier's Practical Advice for Partnering Wine with Food*

THE ART OF LISTENING

Polishing a tableside manner is done through a combination of training and observing what takes place in the dining room. Sommelier Conrad Reddick encourages all service team members, including those who aspire to join the wine service team, to listen carefully to how he and Molly Wismier talk to the guests about wine. Service team members must focus on the task at hand, but they are to do their best to listen in on the sommeliers' conversations.

The wine service team needs to be acutely aware of what's going on not only at each table but also in the dining room and in the entire restaurant. Trotter calls it "court vision," as in the ability of a basketball player to take in the entire field of play and anticipate what will happen next, à la NBA star Steve Nash and his no-look pass. The player with court vision is always one step ahead of the game. Service people who merely react to situations within a narrow field of vision are unable to fully contribute to the team's success.

"A good sommelier is aware of every dynamic in the room. You have to see everything that is going on. You may be handling the task at hand but you should already be analyzing and preparing for the next one," Trotter says. "One guest may be intently studying every page in the wine list. While at another table, a guest has taken his last sip of wine before the food arrives. Those are important cues. The sommelier must always remember that he or she is a member of the service team. There may even be thirty to sixty minutes an evening when a sommelier is not even dealing with wine."

ANALYZING THE CHESSBOARD

Sommeliers can instantly assess the state of a dining room by, for example, observing the glassware at each table. An empty or nearly empty wine glass, for example, is a signal that the guest is ready for a next course or that the glass needs to be refilled or removed from the table. Glasses are like tea leaves that need to be carefully read by sommeliers and servers. They tell them what needs to be done in that room and what guidance they need to provide the service team in that room as well as what kind of intelligence they need to share with the kitchen. "A smart sommelier needs a sixth sense to accomplish all that needs to be done," says former Trotter's sommelier Linda Violago. "The sommelier must be able to recognize and predict where everything is going. You have to be completely plugged in, and you can't afford to be out of focus or out of step."

When a sommelier is not at a table or orchestrating the flow of service in the dining room, he can gain a wealth of information about the guests' needs or preferences by "lying in the weeds." By hovering on the room's periphery, the sommelier overhears threads of conversations between guests and other service staff that can often be revealing. Once, when Reddick picked up a conversation about how much a guest enjoyed sake while on a trip to Japan, he seized the moment by heading to the kitchen and requesting a special dish to complement sake. A short while later, to the guest's amazement, a glass of sake and a course of steamed tai snapper with tofu and wasabi materialized at the table.

Reddick is constantly listening, watching, and reading the guests in a dining room, allowing him to better anticipate what it might take to enhance the food and wine experience that evening. But he hastens to add, "Intensively observing the guests and their behavior is not meant to be intrusive or an invasion of their privacy.

"I watch carefully to see how a guest responds to a certain question or how a guest reacts to a dish or to a glass or a bottle of wine brought to their table. I might hear them ask: 'What kind of wine is this?' If their tone is negative, I will take the wine away, apologize, and bring them something more to their liking. If the tone of their question is positive, that allows me to better anticipate what they might want next. I might ask them: 'Do you like it? It's a Spanish wine.' Sometimes, guests will want to know why we chose to pair a particular wine with a certain dish, which I'm happy to explain."

Sommeliers at Trotter's essentially interview the wine-drinking guests as they subtly tease out information in the course of a tableside conversation that might reveal clues in suggesting a wine. Guests who are not particularly wine savvy can be more of a challenge. In a case like that, the sommelier might not talk about wine at all, but about the kind of food the guest enjoys. If, for example, the guest says her favorite fruit is an apple, the sommelier may direct her toward a Chardonnay, which has those qualities; a guest who's fond of black pepper and smoked meat could be recommended a Syrah.

Says Reddick, "The interplay between the sommelier and the guest adds to the mystique of our service and elevates the experience for the guest. It impresses them. Our jobs are not to merely transport wine and food to the table."

PROPER PRONUNCIATION

Guests feeling phobic about mispronouncing the name of French or other foreign wines can relax at Trotter's. Even the most sophisticated oenophile may hesitate at reading aloud the label of a European wine in front of a group of dinner partners or business clients. Fear of mispronunciation is one of the great obstacles to ordering wine in a restaurant. But a good sommelier will be sensitive to a guest's anxiety. Take a bottle from Nuits-Saint-Georges, for example. If the guest pronounced it: *new-it saint georges,* Conrad Reddick would know exactly what to retrieve from the cellar. With some guests, a correction of the pronunciation is welcome. On his return to the table, he would be careful *not* to state the appellation (neither the guest's mispronunciation nor the proper pronunciation, *n'wee seng-zhorzh*). Doing either would run the risk of embarrassing the guest. Instead, Reddick might point out other features on the label, such as the vineyard or the vintage, to allow the guest to verify that he is being presented the bottle he ordered. If the guest compliments Reddick on his pronunciation of the features on the label, he might take that opportunity to properly pronounce the name of the wine—but only if he senses that it would be well received by the guest. "Nothing is about us. It is all about the people at the table. What we think and what we know is irrelevant unless a guest asks," he says.

GETTING AHEAD OF THE GAME

The ability to intuitively sense what resources will be needed to blow away a table begins, in many cases, before the guests walk through the door. The restaurant's nightly preservice meetings allow the staff to lay the groundwork for what lies ahead that evening. The meetings often include a critique of the previous night's service—warts and all. The sessions are an opportunity to review the service plan for large tables, which at Trotter's are defined as tables of five or more people. A wine order for a large table, done in consultation with a sommelier in advance of the evening, is reviewed in preservice. Nothing is left to chance.

The meetings also allow chef de cuisine Matthias Merges to review any menu changes and for the sommeliers to discuss any changes in the wine offerings that evening. Much of the information is included in a two-sided handout given to all service team members.

The printout also includes alerts for the evening, which often consist of information gathered by the reservationists about any special needs or requests by the guests. That could include food allergies or the fact that a guest is a vegetarian or pregnant or a returning guest. Anniversaries or birthdays are also often noted on the alert section.

Service team members who recognize the name of a returning guest are encouraged to share with their colleagues at the meeting anything they might recall of the guest's previous visit. For example, a server noted that on a previous visit a guest shared with him that he was thinking of ordering wines of a certain vintage the next time he and his wife dined at the restaurant. Trotter's is fortunate to have a corps of service staff members and leadership team members with ten or more years of experience at the restaurant. Each of them can often recall the preferences of returning guests, who are warmly greeted by name the moment they step through the door.

Using tidbits of intelligence, the wine service team can bring the preferred vintage to the table, much to the delight of the guest. Or it may be the case that the guests were particularly fond of the Champagne on their last visit. With that kind of information swapped at preservice, that guest will be greeted with glasses of bubbly upon their arrival. What might seem like magic to the guest is really nothing more than a strong institutional memory.

STUFF HAPPENS

Trotter's, of course, is a human enterprise, and even the best-trained, best-hired service staff makes mistakes amid the quick-step pace of an evening's service. Glasses are spilled, orders get criss-crossed, servers can collide with food runners, a corked wine is not detected. Sometimes an error or delay is caused by the kitchen. Or the weather may cause a guest to arrive late, possibly throwing service out of sync. "There are unstable and unpredictable variables that interfere with the goal of a flawless experience for the guest," Reddick says.

"In a dining room with fourteen tables, you can have as many as eight to ten different bottles or decanters on the credenza at once during service. It would be easy to pick up the wrong bottle and pour it into a guest's glass. It has happened. We have a system for recording which wine belongs to which table. But mistakes do happen, and when they do we rectify the error by immediately approaching the guest, apologizing, and admitting our fault. We do not point a finger at the person who made the mistake, but accept the blame on behalf of the entire restaurant.

"A mistake means we have failed to deliver for the guest, that we have not met their expectations. I then engage the guest in a conversation to get a sense for how they would like to resolve the matter. We are careful not to say: 'We will do anything to make this up to you' because that may be going too far. You risk losing control of the situation."

On the other hand, Reddick says, a sommelier or server should not throw the problem back in the lap of the guest, essentially saying "It's your problem, tell us what you want done." "They can tell us what they want done and we can provide it, but that means we have only met their request. But we have not exceeded their expectations, which is not our idea of great service. That's mediocre service. The mark of a good restaurant is how adept it is at overcoming mistakes and other challenges. It's possible to impress a guest more by making a mistake and demonstrating to them how sincere you are about correcting it than by simply providing correct service in the first place. The way you recover from an error says something about the restaurant. Any service person in this restaurant cares deeply about the guest and getting it right immediately for them."

Reddick recalls an evening when a guest had shared with the reservationist that it was his girlfriend's birthday and he requested a birthday candle to accompany the dessert course. But he didn't get his wish. The request, which had been recorded in the computer system and mentioned during the alerts at the preservice meeting that night, fell through the cracks. But as the guests were leaving, Reddick suddenly remembered and scrambled to make amends.

He instructed a server to delay the couple's departure while he hightailed it to the kitchen. He explained to the pastry chef how the staff had botched a guest's simple but important request for a candle to cap a romantic dinner. As a special dessert was being prepared, Reddick raced to the cellar to retrieve a bottle of dessert wine.

In a corner of the kitchen, a space was cleared for the special pastry and dessert wine, and this time there was a candle. As the guests were escorted into the kitchen by a server, the lights were dimmed and everyone in the room wished the young woman a happy birthday. Rather than leave the restaurant on a sour note, the couple left on the sweetest of terms.

EXERCISING DISCRETION

One of the hallmarks of Trotter's service is the degree of independence he awards each service person. They are encouraged to make judgment calls without hesitation and to correct a mistake or to elevate an already positive experience. "I have unlimited discretion as a floating sommelier in the restaurant to take responsibility and help solve problems at any table or to do whatever it takes to make that table happy," Reddick explains. Decisions are also made after consultation with colleagues or managers or both.

A sommelier, for example, has the discretion to reduce a bill or waive it entirely if he or she determines that the service was flawed. A sommelier can, at no additional charge to the guest, add an extra bottle or an extra glass of wine, or throw in an additional savory course, a cheese course, or a flight of desserts or dessert wines. A sommelier or a server can present the guest with a gift bag or offer a tour of the kitchen or the cellars.

Sommeliers or servers must account for their value-added decisions by filing a report at the end of the evening that is reviewed by Trotter. If he has questions or concerns he'll discuss it with the service person, but in most cases he is satisfied with the explanation.

Trotter says he has rarely regretted endowing so much decision-making authority in his sommeliers and servers. With the discretion to do whatever it takes to satisfy a guest, a sommelier can quickly decide what needs to be done and then deliver, rather than make the guest wait while he or she consults with upper management. Trotter's advice for leaders at other restaurants: the reward far outweighs the risk.

THE RISK OF ASSUMPTIONS

Sommeliers are especially sensitive to a guest's unease over wine prices. It could be the guest's body language or the way the guest speaks to the sommelier, or it could be the way the guest snaps shut the wine list. A guest might casually instruct the sommelier to order anything they think appropriate, but that can be dangerous territory, as several sommeliers at Trotter's have found. Some guests have complained afterward or on the restaurant's guest satisfaction survey that the sommelier specified an overly expensive bottle of wine, even though the guests essentially gave the sommelier carte blanche in handling their order.

Reddick prefers to establish a rough price range, even if a guest, especially a new one, says he or she is not concerned with the right-hand column on the list. He relies at times on an unwritten formula that guests who have not opted for the Wine Accompaniment or the Premium Wine Experience will be comfortable spending about three-quarters of what they will pay for the meal on wine. So if the meal is $155, the guest will be comfortable with a wine tab in the neighborhood of $115.

Reddick will often spend more time establishing a style and a price range on the first bottle or glass of wine than he will on the next bottle or glass. With the groundwork laid, it's easier to determine an appropriate range for the next bottle or glass.

"A guest might say: 'Let's stay in this range for the bottle of white so we can spend a little more on the red.' Or they might reverse that. You just have to feel it out sometimes. The great thing about having a list like ours is that you can offer the guest such an array of options of styles and price ranges. That helps reduce the possibility of a misunderstanding on price. I can open the list and gesture to the price with my finger without stating it out loud. I will watch the guest's eyes to be certain they are following my direction and watch for their reaction. I can go from there."

TRICKS OF THE TRADE

There are many other steps that Trotter's wine service professionals take to allay any tension. For a business gathering, where there may be six to eight people at a table, a sommelier can discuss price ranges quietly with the host as the other guests carry on with their conversations. The sommelier can guide the guest through the list, mindful of the price range stated. The sommelier can specifically direct the guest to the list's ten-page section of wines under $75.

When the table consists of only a couple or two couples, the task is more delicate because all eyes and ears at that moment are focused on the sommelier. Sometimes the sommelier can stand over the shoulder of the guest with the list and watch as the guest gestures toward certain pages or certain prices. A sommelier's powers of intuition are critical at those moments.

Ultimately, the sommelier tries to get a feel for the style of the wine the guest wants, and price becomes a secondary concern because of the list's breadth of styles and its range of prices. "I am looking for what the guest wants to drink, and we'll get to price later because a guest can get what he or she wants and not be limited by price. Our list has enormous diversity of styles and prices," Reddick says, noting that if a guest wants a bold, fruit-forward red, it doesn't necessarily have to come from Bordeaux but could come from a less celebrated wine-producing region that carries a more modest price tag. Another option is to recommend a leading producer's so-called second label, such as Stag's Leap Hawk Crest.

NO NEED TO APOLOGIZE

There are times when guests, almost apologetically, say they can afford to spend only $50 on a bottle of wine. In a case like that, the sommelier makes no attempt to upsell or dismiss them for their frugality, but assures them they will have a wonderful bottle of wine brought to their table that will pair brilliantly with their meal.

GUEST SATISFACTION SURVEY

What you don't know *can* hurt you. That's why Trotter's invites diners to critique their experience with a guest satisfaction survey that asks about the wine list and the quality of service. Trotter believes every restaurant or any service provider should create a mechanism to collect feedback, be it online or in print form. The process is inexpensive and can provide critical insights.

Since 1990, the satisfaction surveys are presented to diners along with the check at the end of the evening. About half the guests take the time to respond. Some surveys are filled out at the table, some are completed online, and some are mailed back to the restaurant. Trotter says he's received some as long as four years after the guest's dining experience.

The feedback is read carefully by Trotter, who passes the surveys along to the appropriate members of his leadership team. Nine out of ten of the surveys indicate that the guests had a wonderful time. Although he appreciates a compliment, he also suspects some of those who gave their dining experience a glowing review may be holding something back. He says he can count on one hand the number of times in the restaurant's twenty-one-year history that it operated flawlessly.

So he pays extra attention to the 10 percent of the surveys that offer points of criticism. He says if he and his staff don't know what they have done wrong, it will be difficult for them to do things better. Sometimes the criticism is tough to swallow. Christian Giles, who conducts the nightly pre-service meetings, read portions of a three-page letter that a guest attached to his survey. The guest noted that he was generally satisfied with the meal and that he was delighted to meet Charlie Trotter, but added that he felt that some members of the service team that evening appeared to be only half as excited as he and his wife were about the experience.

The critical letter seemed to suck all the oxygen out of the room. After a long pause, Giles urged the staff to put more spring in their step.

Sommelier Conrad Reddick painfully recalls a survey that Trotter passed along to him. The guest was unhappy, claiming that Reddick was pretentious and arrogant. Christian Giles, who manages the front of the house, called the guest to apologize, noting that arrogance and pretension are not part of Reddick's character. Reddick also called to apologize and invite the guest back, assuring him that he and the staff would do everything in their power to craft a delightful evening for them.

The guest, who never did return, was upset that Reddick would not allow him to leave the restaurant with the remains of a large-format bottle that his table was unable to finish. At the time, it was illegal to leave a Chicago restaurant with an unfinished bottle. The law has since been changed to allow opened but properly packaged bottles to be taken out of the restaurant.

The criticism can be fair or unfair, but it must be addressed somehow. There have been times when it was obvious that the service team or the kitchen simply failed to deliver and the guest is comped on a return visit, Trotter says.

The incident notwithstanding, Reddick likes the surveys because they allow him and the wine service team to spot trends. For example, in the course of a month, a handful of guests indicated on their surveys that they believed that the wines on the accompaniment menu were not adequately explained. "At our next wine training meeting, we had a roundtable discussion with the service staff on how we could do a better job of explaining the wine to the guest. What it made me realize was that not everyone was as knowledgeable or enthusiastic about the wines on the accompaniment as they should be."

He shared more research with the staff on each wine and the stories about how and where they were produced. He also encouraged some of the staff members to show more excitement when describing the wine. "When a guest senses that the server or sommelier is excited about the wine, he is more likely to enjoy the wine," Reddick says, who noted that the complaints about the poor descriptions of wines on the accompaniment menu disappeared after the mid-course correction.

Regardless if guests choose a wine from the high end or the low end of the price range, they will get a wine or wines that pair with the food. The sommelier will entertain requests that are seemingly incongruous, such as a red, rambunctious Zinfandel to accompany a delicate, light-bodied fish.

Not all guests are easy to read, however, and that can present a special set of challenges because there is a more limited stream of information between the sommelier and the guest. Reactions to a wine or a dish speak volumes, but when a guest's responses are muted or indifferent, there's less to work with. Uncommunicative or unresponsive guests can frustrate a sommelier or any service staffer who knows his or her role is to interpret information and signals from guests and translate that into an unforgettable evening. But it's best that they not take things personally.

"I'll ask myself if there's something I need to do to get the people at my table excited. Is there something I should say or is there something extra I can offer?" Reddick says. "Or is that just the way the person is? He could be quiet and reserved. A guest is here for three hours and we don't want to poke and prod them every five minutes because that would annoy them. An uncommunicative guest doesn't frustrate me because there are many ways to get a feeling for how his evening is going. You may have to work a little harder and listen more carefully and try to go a little deeper."

TOUGH CUSTOMERS

Much more rare is the cantankerous guest who for some reason sees the evening as an opportunity to be confrontational with the sommelier or the service staff. Reddick recalls a guest who kept complaining that the restaurant had some nerve charging the high prices it did for the wine. "Sometimes, you just have to absorb a guest's unhappiness. You try to kill them with kindness," Reddick says. "I allowed him to explain why he believed our wine prices were out of line. I assured him I was certain that I could find him something at a price point he would find reasonable. In a situation like that you have to be very professional and be careful not to smile because it could be misinterpreted that I was laughing at him."

Unimpressed with Reddick's response, the man departed for the restroom and Reddick returned to his business. The five other guests at the table then gestured for Reddick to return. A woman apologized for her father's bumptious behavior and explained that he has a habit of picking fights with service people every time they take him out to a restaurant. The woman and the others commended Reddick for his gentle handling of their cranky tablemate.

Other guests may be in a fractious mood for reasons that have nothing to do with the restaurant. Regardless of the motive, the sommelier—the person who's ultimately in control of that dining room—must manage the situation.

Reddick says he'll try to preemptively head things off by being an active listener and engaging them in a conversation. "You do have to quell the problem through a dialogue and assure them that we understand their concern and appreciate their feedback. But it's still important to defend the integrity of the restaurant. You don't want to embarrass the guest, but we also have to be considerate of other guests in the dining room. Something like this could intrude on their evening."

"The moment you walk into Trotter's, you get a sense of hospitality, refinement, and sophistication. It's very difficult to do all three."

—Thomas Keller, chef-owner of The French Laundry and Per Se

Just as rare is the intoxicated guest, and it tends to be a guest who arrives at the restaurant already in that state. Trotter's does not serve cocktails or operate a bar. Guests are there for a three-hour dining experience, not a shot and a beer. Generous amounts of water are served to the guest throughout the evening. "We would notice that the moment a guest walks through the door. The receptionist would alert the sommelier and the sommelier would notify the server." The table would be carefully handled. The pace of the meal might be accelerated to concentrate the guest's attention on the meal rather than the wine, and that tactic diminishes the time the guest is in the restaurant. If that guest is loud, a sommelier or a server would stop at the table and say: "[Sir or madam,] we want you to enjoy your evening, but not at the expense of our other guests." In almost every case, Reddick says, the guest gets the message. "There are so many different levels of control at our disposal in that situation. It's not a problem here because we pay such careful attention to our guests. We prevent that from happening." If the situation becomes unmanageable, Trotter himself would ask the guests to leave. That's happened only a handful of times.

SORRY, NO COCKTAILS

Even though guests arrive knowing full well that the restaurant does not serve cocktails, the sommelier or the server still get the occasional request. Reddick will use the opportunity to note that the restaurant does not operate a full bar because it prefers to showcase its renowned wine program. That explanation will usually suffice. Trotter does not serve hard liquor because he believes it numbs the guest's palate, although that's not the reason that will be stated to the guest demanding a cocktail.

Reddick says one table decided to leave when they were informed of Trotter's no-cocktail policy. Only on the rarest of occasions will the rule be bent, such as when one guest argued that for twenty-five years he's started each meal with a vodka martini. Reddick made the accommodation.

While the wine service team finds it more enjoyable to be able to delight its guests by anticipating their needs, they are more than ready to handle the more difficult challenges that can arise at the table.

SERVICE POINTS

Sommeliers at Charlie Trotter's have a knack for anticipating what guests may need rather than simply reacting to their requests. To create a sixth-sense style of wine service, consider these service points:

- Be human. Robotically precise sommeliers make guests uncomfortable. It's not necessary to discuss one's personal life, but a sommelier can score points with a guest by sharing information about his or her professional background. A sommelier, for example, could explain that he or she has been working in the restaurant industry for ten years. That helps make a connection and build a relationship with a guest.

- Read a guest's preferences based on a description of the wines he or she has enjoyed in the past. A guest might, for example, speak fondly of a previous experience with a particular varietal or a wine from a certain region. Or a guest might indicate a preference for a particular style of wine or perhaps a certain vintage.

- Develop "court vision" that allows the great sommeliers to instantly assess the state of a dining room and determine what needs the most immediate attention.

- Listen carefully and study a guest's reaction to questions in order to anticipate what he or she may want next. Don't simply react to requests.

- Get a sense for what the guests would like to know about the wine. It could range from a description of its vinification process to the history of the producers. Some guests may have no interest at all in the wine's back story.

- Admit fault when mistakes happen. Sommeliers should work with the guest to determine how to rectify the problem. Fingers should never be pointed at staff members, even the guilty ones.

- Give sommeliers enormous discretion to compensate for a service mistake, such as waiving a bill, reducing it, or adding extra food or wine courses.

- Subtly determine a wine price range in which the guest will be comfortable to avoid misunderstandings over that sensitive matter.

- Create a special section on the wine list of value-priced offerings.

- Use guest satisfaction surveys to collect customer feedback. Trotter reads every one of them and refers those with complaints to senior managers for resolution.

7

Crafting a World-Class Wine List

Sommeliers at Trotter's have at their disposal an 1,800-selection wine list that Charlie Trotter aptly describes as "an embarrassment of riches" from which they can create an extraordinary experience for the guests.

It's a list of wines that pair exquisitely with the Trotter's cuisine and one that represents all major wine-producing regions of the world. It's a list rich with the classics of Burgundy and Bordeaux and Napa Valley as well some esoteric and eccentric selections. There are wines from all fifty states. And it's a list that changes daily to reflect what's in the $2 million inventory stored in the restaurant's cellars.

The list has had many authors over the course of more than twenty years. It continues to reflect the collective wisdom of Trotter and some of the world's best sommeliers who have crafted the list. Sommelier Conrad Reddick considers it a work of art, appreciated by the restaurant's sophisticated, wine-savvy guests.

"The list is a balance between the great vintages of classic regions and unknown, small-production wineries, certain to be future stars," Trotter explains.

A BLEND OF THE OLD AND THE NEW

The list has evolved from the eight pages of 125 selections representing a $30,000 inventory that Lisa Ehrlich-Giglio created in 1987 to a meticulously organized, sixty-page tome with an encyclopedic breadth. The list has representatives from the traditional wine-growing regions of the Old World as well as selections from many of the up-and-coming regions of the New World, including Chile, New Zealand, and the Willamette Valley in Oregon. One of the goals of the list is to give guests the opportunity to experience something different or unexpected. The leatherbound volume presented to each guest begins with this introduction that reflects Trotter's philosophy on wine service:

"Trotter's list is the best of the best. There is strength in every category. There are multiple vintages of some of the best wines. It is refined, yet has a broad spectrum."

—Fred Dame, Master Sommelier

Each section of this wine list is introduced by a short description of the general characteristics of the wines it contains. We do not attempt to describe the flavors of each wine, but rather give you a reference point with which to orient yourself. Nor do we offer specific selections matched to particular dishes. We believe that food and wine can inspire each other. Here, there are no rules. We believe that the "correct" pairing of a dish with a wine is in large measure determined by the unique tastes of the individual diner.

We do not shy away, however, from suggesting which wines to try, but would rather do it on a personal basis, with your special requirements in mind. Each and every waiter is highly trained to offer advice. Of course, sommeliers are always available if more detailed information is desired.

Fans of the list include the wine judges at the Beverage Tasting Institute. They awarded it the grand prize in the international category two years in a row in *Restaurant Hospitality*'s annual Best Wine Lists in America competition. When Trotter's won in 2005 and 2006, the magazine commented,

> The first place winning wine list, from the internationally renowned Charlie Trotter's has all the "wow" a restaurant could possibly want for some amazing highlights and rarities. As judges, we were impressed by all the selections, the creativity, and the very readable presentation of the list.

> Another feature that really impressed the judges was Trotter's amazing examples of food and wine pairing in the ongoing degustation menus. . . . Going beyond the call of duty, Trotter will even adjust his regular menu on the fly to suit the wine choices of his guests—another rare feat that proves a total commitment to his customers and the ultimate food and wine experience.

The judges particularly like the language used in the introductions to each category on the list. "These introductions are written in a knowledgeable, but friendly and inviting style that conveys a lot of information in a concise and usable way. Using a unique and very personal voice in this way to tell the story of a region."

WHETTING THE APPETITE

Here's an example from the Trotter's wine list that introduces the category on white Burgundy, a favorite of the restaurant:

> The white wines of Burgundy at their finest are the most refined of all white wines on earth. While other chardonnays can equal or surpass even the most robust white Burgundy in power, few of them can rival them in finesse and length, complexity and fascination.
>
> From the northern zones of Burgundy, the steely, mineral-scented wines of Chablis entice with their astonishing length and longevity. They are not the round voluptuous chardonnays one finds in Santa Barbara or South Australia; these are intellectual chardonnays, taut and lean, worthy of reflection.
>
> In the Cote de Beaune, we find silken chardonnays that inspired imitation around the world; the full, broad palate of Corton-Charlemagne, the hazelnut of Mersault, the vanilla and honey Puligny-Montrachet and the citrus Chassagne-Montrachet. These wines give the impression of richness without being heavy or over done.
>
> The fuller wines from these zones can accompany even richer dishes composed of fowl or lobster, and most of the leaner types will amplify the flavors of the seafood.

Each introduction is capped off with an inspirational phrase from writers, royalty, or philosophers ruminating on the subject of wine.

For example, to close the section on Australian red wine, there's this from Socrates: "Nothing more excellent or valuable than wine has been granted by the gods to man."

And there's this light-hearted observation from Madame Lily Bollinger to cap the list's section on Champagne and sparkling wine: "I only drink Champagne when I'm happy, and when I'm sad. Sometimes I drink it when I'm alone. When I have company, I consider it obligatory. I trifle with it if I am not hungry and drink it when I am. Otherwise, I never touch it—unless I'm thirsty."

The famous phrases and poetic verse that speak to wine's glorious history accent Trotter's wine list. There's a rich body of literature on wine that can be tapped to provide the same kind of literary flourish to any wine list.

COVERING THE PRICE SPECTRUM

Prices on the list range from a $25 bottle of Shelton Vineyards Riesling 2003 from the Yadkin Valley of North Carolina to a $35,000 magnum of Château Lafite Rothschild 1870. "We will always have a range of wines that are modestly priced, but we also want to be sure we have some of the big, spectacular wines. Some people want to buy them when they come to a restaurant like this," Trotter says.

The bigger, pricier wines on the list can dazzle the guests, but they can also daunt them. "The price of wine is a sensitive issue, no question about it. There are some pages where the least expensive wine is $550, and that can make some guests uncomfortable and stop exploring the list. So about ten years ago we created a special section in the list of wines that are $75 or less. Our servers and sommeliers can sense when a guest is looking for value on

"The wine list is broad—inclusive rather than exclusive—and gets to as many countries as possible. It also includes some great values, thanks to some shrewd purchasing practices. It also features some wines that are off the beaten path."

—Evan Goldstein, Master Sommelier and author of *Perfect Pairings: A Master Sommelier's Practical Advice for Partnering Wine with Food* the list, and they know to suggest they look at that section where they'll find a variety of interesting, eclectic wines at a lower price point." The wines of $75 or less also appear in the regular pages of the list.

SOME OTHER OPTIONS

There's more than wine on Trotter's wine list. There is a nonalcoholic degustation menu for guests who choose not to drink alcohol. The $45 beverage tasting menu features fruit and vegetable blends, infusions and juices; for example, pineapple and poblano peppers, grapefruit and rosemary, cranberry and ginger, kohlrabi and carrot, pine nut and dried fig, and purple corn and apple. The wine list also includes sake, cognac, brandy, grappa, cordials, and even several artisanal beers.

The rule of thumb in fine dining restaurants is a 200 to 300 percent markup on wine. Trotter says he doesn't follow that formula; in fact, he has no wine pricing formula. "We might buy a $20 bottle of cabernet sauvignon and sell it here for $50. On the other hand, we might buy a 1971 Penfold's Grange, the greatest wine ever made in Australia, for $1,000 and sell it here for $1,400. In terms of a percentage markup, that's fairly modest."

Trotter says several considerations come into play when pricing a bottle; these include its exclusivity and its replacement cost. In most cases, Trotter's wine markup falls within the industry range of 200 to 300 percent. In some cases, however, the restaurant may want to support a favorite winery and offers its wine in the restaurant at

"Twenty years after the restaurant was launched, it continues to push the envelope. Case in point: the restaurant's Premium Wine Experience. Trotter has given himself twice the work to create a unique experience for the guest, which speaks to his restless commitment to perfection."

—Thomas Matthews, executive editor
of *Wine Spectator*

an attractive price with a markup in the range of only 130 to 180 percent. "It's an opportunity to give the wine more exposure, to showcase it."

"When people say our list doesn't have good value, I say that's nonsense. Because our list is all about great value. You can spend $20,000 on a bottle of wine, and it can still be considered a good value. Yes, it's horribly expensive, but still a good value." On the list, of course, are wines by the glass and wines by the half bottle that can keep a selection within a modest budget. Wines by the glass can range from a Montlouis-sur-Loire "Cuvee Touche-Mitaine—Sec" Le Rocher des Violettes 2005 for $8 to a $150 glass of Henschke "Hill of Grace" 1991. Half bottles range in price from Gigondas Château du Trignon 2004 for $24 to a Pauillac Château Mouton Rothschild 1996 for $440.

> "Trotter's wine list is incredible for both its breadth and its depth, and its collection of large-format bottles is one my favorite parts of the wine program."
>
> —Thomas Keller, chef-owner of The French Laundry and Per Se

PLUNDERING THE LIST

But the expensive treasures in Trotter's cellars are there for the asking, and they continue to appreciate at a time when the bull market for fine wine drives prices ever higher. Guests with scholarly levels of knowledge of wine will cherry-pick their way through the list in search of relative bargains. Trotter says,

> For example, we may have bought, ten years ago, a 1945 Château Lafite Rothschild, a first growth, that has been on our list for $6,500, and you can't replace it now for less than $11,000, and we may have forgotten to mark it up to reflect the reality of the market. A collector might recognize that and order it. With rare, older bottles, every time one is opened in the world, the price of every remaining bottle appreciates. The wine

market is dynamic and prices fluctuate constantly. You have to stay on top of it constantly, but it's tough to keep up amid all the other responsibilities. We have been negligent in not keeping track of the value of some of our older wines and not adjusting their value to the actual replacement cost.

The cellars are replenished daily through the restaurant's regular procurement process. The sommelier buys 75 to 80 percent of the restaurant's wine through a network of importers and distributors and occasionally directly from the wine producer. The remaining 20 to 25 percent of the wine is acquired either through auction or, in rare cases, through the acquisition of a private wine collection.

MAKING THE "A" LIST

For many of the top winemakers, landing a spot on one of the world's most renowned wine lists is considered a coup. Many are called but few are chosen. Among those chosen are the more artisanal and cult wine producers who handcraft their wares more in pursuit of passion than of profit.

Conrad Reddick says, "We want to support some of the smaller boutique wineries because they are doing what they do for the same reason that we serve food and wine—we love creating an enjoyable experience for our guests." If he or Trotter senses that a smaller winemaker is passionate about craftsmanship and has a great story to tell, that wine may find its way onto Trotter's list. Many of the winemakers pay Trotter's a visit to share their wine and their stories.

As an example of an artisanal winemaker, there's the Brown Estate, a family-owned winery from the eastern Napa Valley that produces a Zinfandel featured on Trotter's list. Trotter has come to know the family and appreciates their dedication to creating an outstanding Zinfandel.

THE WINE LIST

Here are some fun facts culled from the wine list at Charlie Trotter's:

- *Most Expensive Bottle of Wine (tie):* Château Lafite-Rothschild 1870 (magnum), $35,000; Romanee-Conti Grand Cru Domaine de la Romanee-Conti 1945 (magnum), $35,000.

- *Oldest Bottle of Wine:* Château d'Yquem "Premier Cru Superior" 1857, $12,000.

- *Least Expensive Bottle of Wine:* Penedes "Blanc Seleccio" Can Feixes 2005, $20.

- *Most Expensive Wine by the Glass:* Dom Pérignon Brut 1999, $100.

- *Least Expensive Wine by the Glass:* Tavel Rose Prieure de Montezargues 2006, $9.

- *Largest Bottle of Wine (three-way tie):* Châteaux Lynch-Bages 1989; Château Pichon-Longueville Baron 1989; Drappier Carte d'Or Brut NV. All three are Nebuchadnezzars, which hold the equivalent of twenty standard-size bottles.

- *Longest Description of a Bottle of Wine:* Riesling Kabinett "Longuicher Maximiner Herrenberg" C. Schmitt-Wagner 2005.

KEEPING SCORE

Wine scores and ratings, popular with many guests in evaluating the worth of a wine, have little influence in crafting the wine list at Trotter's. Reddick says he's conscious of the scoring systems of *Wine Spectator* and influential wine critic Robert Parker, but their scores don't dictate what goes on the list.

We are not concerned that a wine is served in other great restaurants or that Robert Parker awarded it a high score. We want
to learn about the wine, its story, then taste it and see if it's
appropriate for our restaurant. Some people say that a good
sommelier is someone who memorizes Parker's scores. He's
respected, but it's only one man's opinion. We have to assess
what is best for the guest. The wine team tastes the wine and
considers for the list the wines that we are excited about. We
base the decision on our opinions, not one critic's opinion. Otherwise, why should we taste any wine?

Just as some guests will base their order on a high price point—
often to impress other guests at the table—some will base their
selection on a rating from Parker. If that's what the guest wants,
that's fine, although Reddick will sometimes probe to determine if
that's the wine the guest truly wants to enjoy with the meal. Ideally,
he says, you want a wine that best fits the guest's tastes, which a
good sommelier can usually determine.

CALLING THE SHOTS

Although sommeliers and servers at Trotter's are intensely interested in determining the right wine for a guest, the guests don't
play a role in authoring the wine list. In fact, Trotter says the degree
of guest influence on the list is zero. "There are guests who will say
we should have a particular wine or a particular vintage on our list,
and we appreciate that, but we don't let the guests determine the
direction of the wine program. It would be like someone going to
the symphony and telling the conductor what music should be
played. When you enter certain environments you put your trust in
the experts and let them make the decisions."

The list has breadth, but it also has great depth in certain
regions such as Bordeaux and Burgundy, which each contribute
about two hundred selections to the list. There's also depth among

California proprietaries, such as Opus One and Dominus, California cabernet sauvignon, and California chardonnay. These special wines pair nicely, which, of course, is a dominant concern at Trotter's.

Sommeliers will sometimes lobby Trotter to have a wine added to the list. In most cases, Trotter will defer to their judgment and the wine will find a spot on the list, although not immediately. Reddick explains that he often allows a newly arrived wine two to three weeks in the cellar to recover from the shock of being transported before it is listed. The rest period allows the sediment to settle.

"The wine list at Trotter's is phenomenal. It's very strong in Burgundy, also in Bordeaux, and there's great strength in Riesling, both French and German. He also has an impressive collection of Austrian wine. I have always been impressed with his collection of large-format bottles. It is spectacular."

—Emeril Lagasse

THE PRICE OF ACCURACY

As a new wine is added to the list, the producer's name, the varietal, the vintage, and other details are scrupulously proofed and reproofed to ensure accuracy. Details are paramount at a place like Trotter's, which prides itself on getting things right. A misspelled word on the list would undermine the restaurant's hard-earned reputation.

Many guests study the list intently either in the restaurant or on the restaurant's Web site prior to dining there. Presenting the list online not only whets the appetite of guests preparing for a visit but also makes the ordering process on the night of the visit more efficient. Guests sometimes arrive with questions that arose as they studied the list prior to their visit.

The wine pages on the Web site www.charlietrotters.com/restaurant/wine are organized by such categories as Champagne, Sparkling Wine, and Wines of the United States. There are categories for white and red with such subcategories as American,

European, Australian, New Zealand, and the Rest of the World. Each page lists the wine's bin number in the restaurant, as some guests prefer to order that way. Also listed are the producer, the vintage, and the price. Pages are visually enhanced with photos from the meticulously appointed cellars or the restaurant's foyer, which greets the guest with a floor-to-ceiling bin of wine.

BREADTH AND DEPTH

Although the list is broad and deep, it can't possibly cover the entire world of wine. There are requests that simply can't be accommodated, says Reddick, who regrets that "there's always going to be something that we'd love to have but don't have on the list. But the list is sixty pages, not six hundred pages." Reddick assures guests that the service staff can usually come very close to matching the wine the guest wants with another alternative from the cellar. He says that if a wine is not on the list, staff will suggest something of a similar profile.

Guests are welcome to bring in their own bottle if it does not appear on Trotter's list. There is a $50 corkage fee. The sommeliers will be just as diligent about matching the cuisine to that bottle as if it were bought from Trotter's.

Ultimately, the wine list is a valuable tool that the sommeliers and service staff can wield to achieve a variety of ends: a glass of Champagne to start an evening, a bottle of cabernet sauvignon to pair perfectly with the cuisine, or a glass of Sauternes to add a sweet, spectacular finishing touch to an enchanted evening.

SERVICE POINTS

Creating a wine list with selections as extensive as Charlie Trotter's is a challenge. Organization is key. These service points should be considered:

- A good wine list strikes a balance between the classics and the up-and-comers, between the Old World and the New World.

- Informative, brightly written sommelier notes, including historical background, serve to introduce each category on the wine list and enhance the guest's experience.

- Rather than use the industry standard 200 to 300 percent markup on wine, Trotter's tends to price its wine on a case-by-case basis and will often reduce its markup to showcase a particular wine or products from a favorite winery.

- Newly arrived wines need to settle for a couple of weeks to overcome any "bottle shock" experienced in transit. Once they've recovered, they can be listed.

- The list must be faultlessly accurate. A misspelled name or word on the wine list suggests that the management is inattentive to the small details. At Trotter's, no single detail is more important than any other.

- Putting the wine list on the restaurant's Web site allows guests to review it prior to their visit.

8

Setting the Stage

From Cellars to Stemware

C harlie Trotter reminds his wine service team that their jobs are 3 percent glamour and 97 percent hard labor. His sommeliers both present and past would hardly disagree with his assessment.

It takes enormous physical stamina to bound countless times each evening up steep, narrow service stairways from the wine cellars to the first and second floor dining rooms or from the kitchen in the back of the house to the foyer in the front. If team members are not retrieving wine, they could be pitching in to run food. On the floor, sommeliers must navigate with an athletic grace through the close quarters of the dining rooms and from table to table, never giving the guest the sense that they are harried or hurried.

The day often begins in the basement cellars or adjoining storeroom where scores of cases of wine have to be stacked, stored, or binned. Cases of wine arrive early each day and are received by veteran morning sous-chef Reggie Watkins, who checks invoices against purchase orders. The cases are stacked in the air-conditioned kitchen and await the arrival of the wine service team, whose members will carry them to the cellars. The wine is never stored in the restaurant's garage or stacked on the rear outdoor deck because the temperature cannot be controlled.

THE SHAPE OF STEMWARE

Elegant stemware provides more than just an aesthetic flair for wine service. Well-crafted stemware is critical in determining how a guest experiences the aroma and taste of a wine. The best wine glasses are engineered to direct the wine to certain taste zones of the tongue. For example, sweetness registers at the tip of the tongue; bitterness at the back. Saltiness is detected near the back of the tongue and acidity near the front. Stemware makers customize the shapes of their glasses to the characteristics of a varietal to accentuate its aroma and taste by maximizing the fruit and integrating acidity or tannins. Tall, slender Champagne flutes are designed to reduce the amount of air to which the sparkling wine is exposed. The greater the air exposure, the less likely the carbonated bubbles will remain active in the glass. No fizz, no fun.

White wine glasses are characterized by rims that taper inward to direct the aroma to the nose, enhancing the flavor. A tulip-shaped Riesling glass can also be used for an off-dry or sweet wine, as it directs the wine toward the front of the palate where sensors of sweetness are located. Slightly larger than white wine glasses are red wine glasses, with their rounder bowls that allow the wine drinker to better appreciate the bolder aromas of a red. The broader bowls allow the wine to aerate, to open up and become more expressive. The Riedel Sommeliers series, for example, has more than ten stems, including Burgundy-Pinot Noir, White Burgundy, Bordeaux-Cabernet, and Vintage Champagne. Trotter's assiduously trains its front-of-the-house staff to be able to recognize the different stems so that each wine always goes in the right glass.

EVERY PIECE IN ITS PLACE

In advance of an evening's service, stemware must be moved from floor to floor or from room to room to ensure that there's a proper balance throughout the restaurant and to reduce any unnecessary movement during the heat of battle. The Sommeliers series stemware—the delicate Riedel crystal that is used for the Premium Wine Experience—is hand washed in a sink in the foyer and carefully polished.

Hundreds of containers of bottled water must be moved from basement storage to the second-floor cellar, the bar must be stocked and equipment such as ice buckets and decanters repositioned in the restaurant after all the activity of the night before. Not all the work entails heavy lifting. The wine that lines the bins of the cellars must be procured, a process that can take five hours a day a couple of days a week—all in advance of service. The wine list is updated daily to reflect new arrivals and selections that are no longer available.

When the party's over, 150 to 200 wine bottles emptied during the course of service are assembled in the kitchen and catalogued against inventory to ensure that everything was rung in properly. The bottles are recycled. It's time to go home. By 2 A.M., the day that began around noon has come to an end; along the way the sommeliers have described for their guests and poured some of the most wonderful wines in the world in one of the top wine destinations in America. It's that 3 percent that makes the other 97 percent of the job worthwhile.

None of the wine service team members diminish the importance of the other 97 percent. Without a meticulously organized cellar, a smartly managed inventory, a well-maintained supply of stemware, and a wine list that always reflects some of the world's best offerings, the glamorous 3 percent sliver of their jobs would not exist.

PRIMING THE PUMP

The wine that flows into the restaurant is the result of a long-established procurement system that occupies many of the sommeliers' nonservice hours. Sommelier Conrad Reddick spends Monday afternoons when the restaurant is closed and a couple of afternoons prior to the evening's service speaking on the phone or swapping e-mail with wine distributors or importers, which supply the lion's share of the wine served in the restaurant. Using his negotiating skills, he works to get the best deals possible for the restaurant and its guests.

Representatives of the importers or distributors also make appointments to bring their wares to the sommeliers at the restaurant to earn a coveted spot on the list. The wines procured from the importers and distributors carry price tags in the restaurant of about $75 to $200 a bottle, the most popular range. If a distributor or importer does not carry a particular wine sought by the restaurant, the sommelier may seek it directly from the winery and, if necessary, make arrangements for the winery to move it through a local distributor to get it to Trotter's door.

The more expensive or more exotic wines that grace the list are sometimes bought by way of wine auction houses such as Hart Davis Hart or Acker Merrall & Condit. The auction houses typically alert potential buyers with an e-mail blast announcing an allotment they have acquired through, for example, an estate in France.

I'LL TAKE EVERYTHING

Reddick reviews the e-mail from the auction houses in search of wines that are running low on the list or for new offerings to enhance the list. A wish list is forwarded to Trotter, who may reject the request or suggest that only certain wines be procured or that the purchase order be reduced from $20,000 to $12,000. Or he may instruct his sommelier to buy the entire lot. "That's always fun, to call the dealer and say, 'We want to buy the entire Sauternes lot you sent us. We'll take it.' And when they ask us what exactly we want, I say 'We want everything.'"

Private collectors will occasionally offer to sell the contents of their cellar to Trotter's, but the offer is rarely considered because the restaurant does not have the time to assess the state of the collection's storage or to conduct an appraisal. The restaurant prefers to leave that up to the auction houses.

As with any purchasing process, the cost of each case, half case, or bottle is recorded on the restaurant's computer network and invoices are referred to the restaurant's accounting specialists for payment.

> "Trotter has continuously upgraded the cellars over the years to optimize storage conditions. A bottle is only as good as the environment in which it is stored."
>
> — Thomas Matthews, executive editor of *Wine Spectator*

Wine orders come in throughout the week, and when they do, members of the wine service team must find a place for the new arrivals. The invoice that accompanies a new case or half case is double-checked in the cellar to be sure the distributor has sent the right shipment and the price is right.

If all's well, the cases and half cases are broken down and the bottles' labels, both front and back, are carefully examined to ensure proper placement of the bottle in the bin system, which numbers from 1 through 3,400, with most of them in use. Labels are carefully studied to be certain they are properly classified in the cellar and correctly spelled and categorized once they appear on the wine list. New World wines are listed by the producer, Old World by the region. The numerically organized bins are not static. They are frequently shifted and reconfigured—while still maintaining the numerical structure—to maximize space in the cellar's close quarters.

NEATNESS COUNTS

A misspelled name on the wine list can be an embarrassment, especially when a guest hails from a region in which the wine is produced. Binning can be repetitive and tedious, so it requires a high degree of concentration to be sure that the seemingly little things are done right, Reddick says.

During wine service training, the entire service team is occasionally brought to the cellars and instructed on how to locate a wine. In one training drill that smacks of a scavenger hunt, the sommelier-instructor will give students a laundry list of wines to locate. The sommelier will watch intently as the staffer pulls a wine from a bin to ensure that it is being done correctly.

Any member of the service team may need to visit the cellars during the course of an evening, although the sommeliers and the food runners are the ones who must frequently pull wine. In training sessions, sommeliers explain that wine from a bin is pulled from top to bottom and from left to right—similar to the direction in which English and the European languages are read on a page.

The bottle on the bottom row in the far right-hand corner carries a red dot, indicating that is the last bottle of its kind in the bin. The red dot is designed to alert the service team that it's the last one.

> "It's hard to imagine how Trotter's can take it to another level. He has an incredible collection of stemware and decanters, the wine is always served at the right temperature, and I've never had a corked wine there."
>
> —Thomas Matthews, executive editor of *Wine Spectator*

GUIDING THE GUESTS

Because the cellars are showpieces for the restaurant, certain wines are put on special display amid the red cedar bins. Any member of the restaurant staff, including chefs, can bring a guest to the cellars and let them ooh and aah at one of the world's best wine collections. Leading a tour takes time away from responsibilities on the floor or in the kitchen, but a colleague instinctively knows how to pick up the slack for the staffer leading a guided tour.

Among the highlights of any cellar tour is the restaurant's vertical (in a series of consecutive vintages) collection of Château Mouton Rothschild, a first-growth Bordeaux. The rows begin with the 1945 vintage. Sommeliers say guests often ask to be shown the most expensive bottles in the cellars. Guides point to such treasures as a 1921 Petrus, a Lafite Rothschild from 1870, and a Romanée-Conti—a Burgundy that would cost the guest $35,000.

Honoring a European tradition, the cellars also contain the private collections—some valued at up to $75,000—of wine connoisseurs who frequently dine at the restaurant. A sommelier will draw from the connoisseur's special collection as he or she crafts a wine list and consults with the kitchen in preparing that guest's dining experience.

TROTTER'S TO GO

The wine selection is much less extensive, and the prices are not nearly as expensive. The ambience is not as rarefied, but the service is what you would expect from Trotter's—attentive and gracious.

Trotter's To Go, the retail outlet less than a mile from the restaurant, has been described as Trotter's experiment in translating his food and wine into an accessible neighborhood shop. Since its opening in 2000, the store has been well received by residents and people willing to travel a ways to get a taste of Trotter's at prices comparable to a deli's.

The shop features about 250 different selections of wine, with prices ranging from $7 to $400 a bottle. The staff at the shop, which is a cross between a gourmet shop and the deli section of one of the local grocery stores, is just as eager to help customers find the right match between food and wine as the wine service team is in the restaurant.

Mark Signorio, who manages the store, says customers at wine retailers or gourmet shops won't get the same level of service they do at Trotter's To Go. "We have taken Charlie Trotter's passion for food, wine, and great service and brought it to the retail level."

As an example of the go-the-extra-mile brand of service patented in the restaurant, Signorio says if a customer seems hesitant about purchasing a new product, the staff will instinctively provide a sample. The walls on the wine side of the shop are lined with bottles in bins that are organized by body type and flavor profile.

For example, there is a section for crispy, racy whites and another for juicy, fruity reds. And within each section the bottles are arranged by geography. The New World reds sections go from Oregon's Willamette Valley in the north to New Zealand in the south.

There's also a display called the sommelier's selection of higher-end wines chosen by the restaurant's wine team. A bottle's label is much more important at retail than it is in a restaurant where a sommelier will describe a bottle, Signorio says. And there are other merchandising considerations that don't come into play in the restaurant; these include playing to the consumer's sweet spot—a marketing concept that says retail customers are more apt to pay special attention to items on store shelves that are between a customer's forehead and knee level.

However, Signorio always likes to put an interesting wine or two above or below the sweet spot to make sure customers are taking in the entire selection. The shop hosts free tastings every Friday and impromptu sessions throughout the week. The tastings often have a regional theme such as Italian, French, or blends from the New World. The shop also hosts book signings.

Leveraging the Trotter's name, the store is able to get wines that distributors and importers don't normally make available to retailers, according to Signorio.

The store and the restaurant have separate facilities and separate staffs, but in addition to the name on the doors there is some synergy between the two. Guests at the restaurant who enjoyed a particular wine may ask where they could buy one. The sommeliers will refer them to the store.

Do customers of Trotter's To Go become guests at the restaurant? Signorio says that's not usually the case. "It's actually the other way around, although I have had customers come in here before their first visit to the restaurant. I explain to them to be specific about the wine they want to drink that night and I tell them they shouldn't be intimidated by the wine list nor should they hesitate to ask questions of the sommelier. I say: 'They are there to help you. Their job is to make the wine approachable and fun for the guest. That's what food and wine is all about. It's a celebration.'"

BEAUTY HAS ITS PLACE

To ensure that the investment is well maintained, the cellars are temperature- and humidity-controlled. The red wine cellar is at a constant 59 degrees, the white wine cellar at 52. Consistently maintaining those levels can be difficult in the basement of a century-old building, but the wine service team is responsible for keeping the cellars in pristine condition. "The quality of the cellars is never sacrificed," Reddick says. "My predecessors made sure that these cellars were a thing of beauty." The cellars are lovingly cared for on a daily basis by the wine service team. Floors are immaculate, bottles are dusted. Everything is in its proper place.

Trotter says the cellars are designed, first and foremost, to be functional. "The aesthetics of the cellars are important, but they are secondary to the proper maintenance and storage of the wine. Some of the wines have been down there five years or more. It's a big investment."

Trotter notes that cellaring the wine and seeing that it ages properly is not an easy proposition. "For example, we have some younger wines that are not going to age well beyond two or three years. They begin to lose their edge after that, and that's something our sommeliers have to be mindful of. As we approach that point and the bottles are still in the bins, we might have to begin pouring those wines by the glass at a break-even price point rather than forfeit the value of those bottles."

In other words, there are substantial risks to the rewards of a cellar, aesthetically pleasing or otherwise. But Trotter has always opted for an attractive look to the cellars because, for many guests, a visit to them can add the perfect finishing flourish to an evening.

> "Charlie Trotter has never taken a second seat to anyone in terms of the quality of his stemware, the decanters, and proper refrigeration of the wine."
>
> —Emeril Lagasse

ADDING THAT EXTRA TOUCH

Trotter says, "To get a truer sense for what the guest would appreciate, I sometimes ask myself: 'What would I like if I went to a restaurant?' I have a professional interest in seeing a restaurant's wine cellar, of course, but I suspect many guests would enjoy a tour. It doesn't take much additional effort on our part, but it can make a big difference for the guest." Trotter believes that every restaurant should provide its guests behind-the-scenes access to its kitchen or wine cellar or both because it heightens the guests' experience. Nothing at Trotter's is off limits to a guest. Guests who have requested a peek at Trotter's second-floor office are escorted to his book-lined sanctuary.

"Our sommeliers or servers might say at the end of the evening: 'Would you like to see our cellars?' And the guest will say: 'Oh, is that even possible? We would love to do that.'"

Short, guided tours to the cellars, the kitchen, and the studio kitchen where Trotter's public television program is produced also create a sense of transparency in the restaurant. "I believe in demystifying things for the guest. In a bygone era of fine dining, the guest was never allowed to peek behind the curtain. It was forbidden. It was very European. But we are uniquely American, so we take them to the cellars or down the hot line of the kitchen on a busy night. We are very proud of the way our team conducts itself, and we are eager to show our guests what goes on behind the scenes. We are delighted to show off our cellars and our kitchen. I think it's good for both our guests and our staff."

SERVICE POINTS

Sommeliers at Charlie Trotter's are also the cellar masters, and as such they are responsible for the restaurant's impressive collection of stemware—assets that require savvy management. Consider these service points:

- Bring service team members to the cellars during training sessions to rehearse finding particular bottles. That familiarizes the staff with the binning system in the cellars, allowing them to efficiently locate a bottle.

- Offer guests tours of the cellars by sommeliers and other employees. It's a memorable way to cap a guest's evening.

- Protect the wine investment with temperature and humidity controls in each cellar.

- Invest in top-of-the-line stemware to underscore the establishment's reverence for the wine. The benefits of the delicate stemware outweigh the high cost of its breakage.

CONCLUSION

At Charlie Trotter's, the sommelier is more than the manager of the restaurant's primary profit center, more than a connoisseur who can artfully pair wine with food, and more than an expert on the world of wine.

The sommelier must be the best service person in the house. And that's a particularly tall order at a house that's made itself synonymous with exquisite service and wine service. A member of the wine service team at Trotter's must have a skill set as broad as it is deep. It's a set of skills that must be continuously honed to meet the ever-evolving needs of the guests and the restaurant.

A sommelier at Trotter's must have the ability to:

- *Scan the room,* even the entire restaurant, and instinctively determine what needs to be done next. The sommelier reads such tea leaves as water levels in glasses or how a table is reacting to a dish. Trotter calls it "court vision."

- *Read a guest.* Using his or her powers of perception, the sommelier can discern the guest's needs, often through a dialogue in which the guest reflects on previous dining experiences. Listening skills are paramount.

- *Anticipate.* Guests are not always able to articulate what they truly want. The great service people don't merely react to requests from a guest; they develop a sixth sense for what the guest may want next.

- *Navigate.* The sommelier, even though not at any particular table-side for the entire evening, must be able to guide the guest through a three-hour dining experience. The sommelier must take complete ownership of the table.

- *Operate with style and grace.* The sommelier must be conscious of the guest's space and should minimize motion in the guest's immediate vicinity. The job requires enormous physical stamina.

- *Taste.* A sommelier's discerning palate can help protect a guest from a wine that is corked or is not true. The sommelier can also help protect the reputation of the winemaker by recognizing a bottle that falls short of the winery's standards.

- *Cooperate.* The sommelier must exercise tact when working with the kitchen. Heavy-handed requests of the kitchen will not be well received, even in a kitchen that's known for redirecting a course for the sake of the wine.

- *Lead.* The general service staff looks to the sommelier for guidance in the dining room amid the press of service. The sommelier must be able to direct the flow of service in a dining room or even the entire restaurant.

- *Inspire.* Sommelier Conrad Reddick says one of the most important parts of his job is getting the wine service and general service team excited about the wine and food that they are serving. If he fails to convey a sense of enthusiasm to the staff, then he has failed as a manager.

- *Mentor.* The best sommeliers take the time to share their wisdom and experience with less experienced staffers. They point out faults and applaud a sincere effort.

- *Accept criticism.* Trotter demands the best and doesn't hesitate to let a sommelier know if his or her performance is lacking. Comments in the guest satisfaction surveys can be candid and harsh, but they alert the service team to things that need to be done better.

- *Admit mistakes.* They happen, even at Trotter's. But sommeliers need to recover from a mistake, regardless if it was committed by the sommelier or a coworker, by never pointing fingers and by working with the guest on steps to make it right.

- *Negotiate.* Sommeliers procure the wines and manage the cellars. They need to know the market, pricing trends, and how to economically fill the cellars.

- *Represent the restaurant.* The sommelier is, in many cases, the face of the restaurant during service and during special events. He or she must be an articulate spokesperson for the restaurant.

- *Organize.* The sommelier is responsible for the wine list and for training the wine service and general service staff in how to use it. Weekly training sessions must have a sharp focus and a clear objective.

- *Master the art of hospitality.* For some guests, wine can be an uncomfortable subject: it's expensive, it's hard to pronounce, and there's so much to know. But a good sommelier can cut through all the trepidation and make a guest feel at ease. It's the mark of a gracious host.

The list of skills is long, and it may seem like a lot to ask of someone, but Trotter provides his sommeliers with a raft of resources that allow them to succeed. Their operating platform is the restaurant's 1,800-selection wine list that includes some of the greatest wines in the world. The wines are not there for trophy purposes. It's a working list, and the sommeliers are allowed to taste the great wines that flow into the restaurant.

They work in a restaurant where they are respected by their colleagues in the kitchen and can expect the chefs to accommodate their requests to adapt the cuisine to the wine they are pouring. The sommelier-chef relationship is strong. Trotter has always made it a priority.

He spares no expense to train his sommeliers. They have the opportunity to spend time with some of the world's leading winemakers who come, at Trotter's invitation, for special events at the restaurant. His sommeliers travel all over the country to meet the best winemakers and spend time in their vineyards and wineries.

In turn, Trotter expects his sommeliers to be master teachers. In training sessions he allows them to open bottles that the restaurant could sell for hundreds of dollars.

Trotter's sommeliers work with the best stemware and decanters available. When the stemware breaks—as some inevitably does—the restaurant orders more.

Trotter vests his sommeliers with the discretion to do whatever it takes to create an extraordinary dining experience for the guest. It's "no questions asked" when a sommelier adds an extra course, an extra glass, or an extra bottle to elevate the experience for a guest. His sommeliers are confident and self-assured.

And when the graceful tango between the service staff and the guest is flawlessly executed, the perfect night of service has been achieved.

APPENDIX
Seasonal Food and Wine Pairings

To illustrate the inspired partnerships between food and wine at Charlie Trotter's, we take a look at four grand menus and the wines that are paired with each course from the Wine Accompaniment of that evening. Menus have been selected from each of the four seasons. The sommeliers have provided brief comments on each of the food-and-wine pairings.

SPRING

FOOD: Coromandel Bay Oyster with Cockles & Yuzu
WINE: Philipponnat "Royale Reserve" Brut NV
COMMENT: Flavors of each are clean with a touch of saltiness.

FOOD: Tasmanian Ocean Trout with Orange Rind, Fennel Pollen & Trout Roe Vinaigrette
WINE: Bonny Doon "Ca' del Solo" Albarino, Monterey 2006
COMMENT: The wine offers notes of ripe fruit, sweetness, and acidity that complement the dish's citrusy flavors from the orange rind. The Albarino resists overwhelming the light, herbaceous tones of the trout.

FOOD: Alaskan Black Cod with Picholine Olives, Artichokes & Stinging Nettles

WINE: Franz Hirtzberger "Rotes Tor" Gruner Veltliner Smaragd, Wachau 2005

COMMENT: The richness and saltiness of the cod are an appetizing match with the wine's roundness and full-bodied feel. Alcohol content is high and the oak's influence is neutral.

FOOD: Arkansas Rabbit Loin & Leg with Turnips, Fingerling Potatoes & Mustard Greens

WINE: Isabel Estate Pinot Noir, Marlborough 2004

COMMENT: The meat is lean and delicate, but the potato is rich tasting. It's countered by the wine's acidity and the astringency of the moderately high level of tannins.

FOOD: Summerfield Farm Lamb Shoulder with Garlic, Aged Manchego & Parsley

WINE: K Vintners "Cougar Hills" Syrah, Walla Walla 2005

COMMENT: The tannins and the ripe fruitiness of the wine play well off the sweetness of the garlic and the saltiness of the lamb.

SORBET COURSE (no wine pairing): Cantaloupe with Feta Cheese & Spearmint

FOOD: Organic Buttermilk with White Pepper, Toasted Milk Ice Cream & Nutmeg

WINE: Tokaji-Aszu "5 Puttonyos" Château Pajzos 1999

COMMENT: The dessert's texture is rich, sweet, and creamy. The concentrated sugars from this botrytized wine make for a delightful pairing. The wine's sweetness also contrasts with the dish's white pepper influences.

FOOD: Olive Oil Ice Cream with Venezuelan Chocolate & Red Wine

WINE: Bodegas Toro Albala "Don PX—Gran Reserva" Pedro Ximenez, Montilla-Moriles 1971

COMMENT: This older wine is fortified for sweetness and has nuances of nuttiness that pick up the dessert's nutty, dried fruit character.

SUMMER

FOOD: Amuse Gueule

WINE: Egly-Ouriet "Ambonnay—Grand Cru" Brut Non Dose NV

COMMENT: The Champagne is served cold, which accentuates its crispness and acidity and goes beautifully with the *amuse*. This pair launches the evening on a bright, effervescent note.

FOOD: Japanese Hamachi with Roasted Bell Pepper, Kalamata Olive Sorbet, Spanish Paprika & Basil Oil

WINE: Rudi Pichler "Wachauer" Gruner Veltliner Federspiel, Wachau 2004

COMMENT: The *hamachi*'s style is clean, almost raw, as it is poached at a low temperature. It is delightfully paired with a wine that is clean, lightly spiced, and low in alcohol.

FOOD: Alaskan Halibut with Chives, Dungeness Crab & American Sturgeon Roe

WINE: Riesling Kabinett "Longuicher Maximiner Herrenberg" C. Schmitt-Wagner, Mosel 2004

COMMENT: This one is complicated because of the dish's tapestry of flavors. The halibut is rich and fleshy, the crab is sweet, and the sturgeon is salty. But the pairing with the Riesling Kabinett is superb thanks to the wine's presence of acid, absence of oak, and sweet undertone.

FOOD: Whole Roasted Squab with Braised Sweet Onions, Chanterelle Mushroom & Szechwan Peppercorn Reduction

WINE: Movia Pinot Nero, Brda 2001

COMMENT: With a hint of mushroom, the wine plays smartly off the meaty quality of the chanterelle mushrooms in the dish.

FOOD: Four Story Hill Dry Aged Angus Strip Loin with Kohlrabi, White Runner Bean, Pickled Garlic & Spiced Date

WINE: Moss Wood Cabernet Sauvignon, Margaret River 2001

COMMENT: The Australian wine's vegetal style is an appetizing match for the dish's riot of vegetables.

SORBET COURSE (no wine pairing): Meyer Lemon & Olive Oil Sherbet with Candied Lemon Peel

FOOD: Poached Rhubarb with Jasmine Semifreddo & Celery

WINE: Bodegas Gutierrez de la Vega "Casta Diva—Cosecha Miel" Muscat, Alicante 2003

COMMENT: Floral and vegetal notes in both the food and the wine make for a perfect pairing.

FOOD: Chocolate Mignardises

WINE: Quinta do Crasto Port 1999

COMMENT: Chocolate and vintage Port. It's a classic fine dining dessert.

FALL

FOOD: Amuse Gueule

WINE: Gaston Chiquet "Tradition—Premier Cru" Brut NV

COMMENT: This traditional autumnal pairing will excite the palate and set the table for the courses to follow.

FOOD: Poached Skate Wing with Red Curry, Twenty Four Hour Braised Fennel, Razor Clams & Herb Oil

WINE: Lugar de Cervera Albarino, Rias Biaxas 2005

COMMENT: The light, clean, delicate dish with a touch of spice from the red curry pairs happily with the wine's freshness thanks to its moderate acid and lack of oak.

FOOD: Alaskan Halibut with Sweet & Sour Duck Gizzards, Crosnes, Battera Kombu & Watermelon Radish

WINE: Chassagne-Montrachet "Les Blanchots-Dessous" Marc Morey 2004

COMMENT: The dish combines a variety of influences: earthiness, richness, acidity, and the clean taste of the halibut. The wine's acidity, touch of oak, and earthiness combine with the dish to create an elegant pairing.

FOOD: Monk Fish Tail with Crispy Hominy, Huitlacoche, Zucchini, Rosemary & Red Wine Veal Essence

WINE: Yabby Lake "Mooroduc" Pinot Noir, Mornington Peninsula 2004

COMMENT: Red wine with fish? Trotter's says yes, especially when the fish is roasted and accompanied by the earthiness of hominy, the vegetal notes of zucchini, and the truffle-like pungency of *huitlacoche*. The Australian Pinot has a roasted, smoky tone of its own, but its silky texture won't overwhelm the dish.

FOOD: South Dakota Bison Tenderloin with Quinoa, Black Cardamom Mole & Ash Baked Eggplant

WINE: Mendel "Unus," Mendoza 2004

COMMENT: The Malbec from Argentina has the tannins to cut through the bison. The wine's ripe fruit plays deliciously off the cocoa in the dish's mole sauce.

SORBET COURSE (no wine pairing): Oloroso Sherry Sorbet with Dates & Mustard Greens

FOOD: Honey Crisp Apple with Toasted Caraway, Maytag Bleu Cheese & Cider Gelée

WINE: Kracher "TBA No. 1—Nouvelle Vague" Zweigelt, Burgenland 1998

COMMENT: One inviolable rule of pairing: The dessert wine needs to be sweeter than the dessert. This rosé, with just a touch of tannin, is just that.

FOOD: Chocolate Mignardises

WINE: Smith-Woodhouse Vintage Port 1985

COMMENT: The classic combination of chocolate and port puts a sweet finishing touch on any meal.

WINTER

FOOD: Amuse Gueule

WINE: Philipponnat "Royale Reserve" Brut NV

COMMENT: The Champagnes change with the season. This rich-tasting sparkler has a hint of smokiness and seems just right for the start of a cold winter's night.

FOOD: Poached Kampachi with Red Curry, Twenty Four Hour Braised Fennel, Razor Clams & Herb Oil

WINE: Santiago Ruiz "O Rosal" Rias Baixas 2005

COMMENT: The dish and the wine from Spain's province of Galicia share the table amicably thanks to the herbaceous nuances of both. The wine's crisp acidity accents the dish.

FOOD: Hawaiian Walu with Sweet & Sour Duck Gizzards, Crosnes, Battera Kombu & Watermelon Radish

WINE: Auxey-Duresses Comte Armand 2004

COMMENT: The dish is rich and earthy and marries well with the richness and acidity of the wine. The fruit is ripe and there's a distinct earth component.

FOOD: Whole Roasted Squab with Huitlacoche, Zucchini, Rosemary & Pig's Feet

WINE: Joseph Swan "Trenton" Pinot Noir, Russian River 2002

COMMENT: The wine is robust and dense in color and has moderate levels of tannin that allow it to stand up to this dish.

FOOD: Venison Loin with Quinoa, Black Cardamom Mole & Ash Baked Eggplant

WINE: Antiyal Valle del Maipo 2004

COMMENT: The dish and the wine are particularly well suited for each other because of elements of smokiness, meatiness, and chocolate in each.

SORBET COURSE (no wine pairing): Oloroso Sherry Granite with Dates & Mustard Greens

FOOD: Organic d'Hiver Pears with Caramelized Endive & Burnt Hickory Syrup Ice Cream

WINE: Kracher "TBA No. 1—Nouvelle Vague" Zweigelt, Burgenland 1998

COMMENT: The light tannins of this rosé play magnificently off the bitterness of the endive and the earthiness of the burnt hickory.

FOOD: Chocolate Mignardises

WINE: Warre's Late Bottled Vintage 1995

COMMENT: Chocolate and a late harvest wine make for a sweet finishing treat to an extraordinary evening.

INDEX